Handbook for Healthy Living with a Mood Disorder

STEPHEN NAWOTNIAK, OTR/L

TRUE DIRECTIONS
AN AFFILIATE OF TARCHER BOOKS

HANDBOOK FOR HEALTHY LIVING WITH A MOOD DISORDER

iUniverse books may be ordered through booksellers or by contacting:

iUniverse
1663 Liberty Drive
Bloomington, IN 47403
www.iuniverse.com
1-800-Authors (1-800-288-4677)

Because of the dynamic nature of the Internet, any web addresses or links contained in this book may have changed since publication and may no longer be valid. The views expressed in this work are solely those of the author and do not necessarily reflect the views of the publisher, and the publisher hereby disclaims any responsibility for them.

Any people depicted in stock imagery provided by Thinkstock are models, and such images are being used for illustrative purposes only.
Certain stock imagery © Thinkstock.

ISBN: 978-1-4917-2544-3 (sc)
ISBN: 978-1-4917-2545-0 (e)

Library of Congress Control Number: 2014903707

Printed in the United States of America.

iUniverse rev. date: 3/21/2014

Believe you can, believe you can't. Either way you are right.
—Henry Ford

Contents

1. Understanding Myself 1

An individual with a mood disorder will often ask, "What is the difference between me and the disorder?" and "What is really me?" This chapter starts the book with a person-centered approach supporting you in defining yourself separately from your condition. The focus of the chapter is on being the creator of the person. Interests, goals, likes, and dislikes are distinguished. Roles and their missions are established as cornerstones to live out while experiencing symptoms.

2. Understanding My Condition 17

This chapter guides you in understanding your diagnosis and how it presents itself in your life. It helps you to understand the needs and qualities of your disorder as an entity instead of an illness. If we can understand our condition's characteristics, we can better accommodate its needs and build a relationship with it.

3. Creating the Structure **41**

In this chapter, we work to create an external structure to support you in living out your internal priorities during times of mood disorder. You create a personalized template identifying your most productive times and groggy times, match an activity with the appropriate time, and identify and develop daily and weekly priorities. This process is used to create a plan to follow during times of emotional storms.

4. Building Relationships **55**

Human beings are social creatures, and as such, we exist in relationships. Be it with the self, an individual, a community, or the divine, we share and receive. This chapter will support you in distinguishing some of the specific tools that influence and make up a relationship so that you can better influence its quality. I don't claim that these will make everything okay. I simply share that they are important skills in the process of developing and living relationships.

5. General Finances **65**

Finance is a true source of stress for anybody when mismanaged and can be further intensified when the brain is in a compromised state. In addition, the various emotional states consistent with a mood disorder can affect an individual's objectivity, leading to long-term consequences of poor decisions. This chapter supports you in developing a system to help protect your money from the impulse buying of mania and missed-bill deadlines of depression. Activities are used to organize expenses and create a realistic awareness of your current financial situation.

I have included some postings from my blog to share my thought process during the intense *passion* associated with the diagnosis, as well as additional resources and web addresses of sources I have found helpful in my journey.

Some Posts from my blog: http://sharingthejourney.postagon.com/

Professional Advisory from an Occupational Therapist

This is *not* an *evidence*-based program, as I do not have objective data from a large pool of participants (or *n* in statistical terms) to validate the specific tools and techniques outlined in this book. It is *experience*-based, sharing the skills and tools I have found to work for me through the *application of various approaches*. The book before you is the culmination of my experiences: good and bad, successes and failures, victories and defeats, objective data and lived experience. It represents the best tools and techniques I use to successfully live my bipolar experience at this time. I have found that "it works for me" is the best evidence for me to choose the tools that support me in designing, living, and experiencing a desired quality of life. As an occupational therapist, *I believe in the importance of evidence-based research* as a foundation to guide the selection and application of tools and techniques, *not limit* the options to select from. I believe that the true use of evidence-based treatment is to draw information from research studies, lived experiences of consumers, lived experiences of families, *and* expert opinions, synthesizing *all* information into an educated opinion, and then provide a selection of options to choose from. *Individual progress* is the evidence I follow to sustain the program, and it is the *why* behind the sharing of this book.

My Story

Twelve years ago I was diagnosed with bipolar disorder after a weeklong hospitalization for a severe case of depression and have been coping with the symptoms and in the process of recovery ever since. Today, and forever forward, I fully embrace that I live with a bipolar condition. I am an occupational therapist, have been so successfully for three years, and have developed skills and systems to address my needs and successfully live a desired quality of life. Do I experience the volatility of emotions consistent with the diagnosis? Absolutely. Does this emotional volatility and intensity cause me to experience emotional discomfort? Without question. Do I have times I feel that it is a curse and am angry at *God* for having this condition? With great intensity … but I *am not ill*.

I am simply human … an imperfect being requiring skills and tools to accommodate needs and enjoy a desired quality of life.

What are these skills and systems? That is the purpose of this book … to share my personal journey as I developed, used, and shared the specific tools necessary to live a meaningful, purposeful, and desired quality of life *with* a bipolar *condition*.

I offer you my story as a story of *passion*. In May 2000, I set out upon a planned twenty-seven-month nonmotorized trek of service around the United States. This trek had structure and credibility as part of a self-designed master's degree through Buffalo State College and was partially funded as an AmeriCorps project. I shared my message (values of service and education to live a dream) with over one thousand youth and performed over 230 hours of direct community service along the way. I completed an eight- month trek from Buffalo, New York, to Key West, Florida. I had canoed across New York State on the Erie Canal, sailed the Hudson River to New York City on the *Clearwater* (a traditional wooden Hudson River sloop), backpacked to Roanoke, Virginia, via the Appalachian Trail, and then biked from Roanoke to Key West, Florida.

In January 2001, my grandmother passed away and I returned home for the funeral. The trip wasn't over; it would just be modified as it was three times during the three years of planning. My new plan was to do it in sections, returning home to update the website after each leg and update my presentations. I would use that time to secure some speaking engagements and develop a nonprofit organization to raise money for a scholarship and start the Generation TreX scholarship at Clarence Senior High for those students who best exemplified the principles the trek was founded on.

That September, the month I was supposed to leave, was the 9/11 tragedy. My focus shifted from a trek of service to supporting violence-prevention programs in the Buffalo area. I became an AmeriCorps VISTA volunteer and established the nonprofit entity "ACT on Violence Prevention," to provide self-defense-based violence-prevention programming. The board was strong, the programs were loved, and the organization was gathering momentum. But in August 2002, I was hospitalized for acute depression and diagnosed with bipolar disorder.

The next five years were another journey as I learned the nature of the condition, its triggers, and how it showed itself in my life. I felt broken and defeated, ashamed that I had a mental illness. I had forgotten my past accomplishments. It was as though I were leading a completely separate life, second-guessing my abilities, questioning my goals, and trying to develop a sense of control around the life ahead of me.

In an attempt to maintain a life of service, I entered the employment of the Boy Scouts of America, Finger Lakes Council. Thinking I could control my bipolar condition, I lived a high-stress lifestyle that lacked routine. Within a year, my efforts brought me a nomination for Best District Executive in the Northeast Region. But with every up comes a down. We were short-staffed, and the added responsibilities put me in overdrive. A mania surfaced as I attempted to meet and address the increasing demands. I was hit by the depression that always followed my manias. I then had to make one of the toughest concessions of my life. I had to admit that I could not *beat* bipolar. I would have to adapt my life to it. The hardest part of living with bipolar is that the only way to understand how it affects you is through experiencing it. There is no magic pill or book that provides answers. This book merely shares the resources I used as I attempted to put my life back together.

Refusing to give up in my fight against my bipolar condition, I enrolled in New York State's VESID program (Vocational and Educational Support for Individuals with Disabilities). Jack Burrows became my counselor and the single most influential individual in my posthospitalization life. He helped me look at the condition as a teacher instead of as an illness. He helped me forgive myself for having a weakness. He helped me search my soul for the difference I wished to make and guided me to the vocation I am now pursuing: occupational therapy (OT).

OT is a very diverse profession. It focuses on helping individuals achieve their desired quality of life and attain their goals—regardless of medical condition. It's a profession that treats illness and injury as conditions to *accommodate* instead of problems to fix.

Had I known about the profession earlier, I would have pursued it right out of high school. Instead, I was brought to OT by a more circuitous journey. I enrolled in Genesee Community College's Occupational Therapy Assistant program and began rebuilding my life anew as a student. As I began to reassemble the pieces, my two lives began to merge. I began to revisit my projects and positively notice what I had accomplished. Until now, they were but the failures of a guy incapable of reaching his goals. With new hope, I went on to complete my license in Occupational Therapy degree at Utica College where my struggles became an asset.

With every end comes a new beginning. I set off once again on a journey of service but with a greater understanding of myself. I realized that we all carry challenges of some form or another. It is in accepting, understanding, and *embracing* my struggle that I am able to live fully. I must understand the nature of my condition, taking into account its needs as I plan out my life. It is only in satisfying my responsibilities that I have access to the pursuit of my dreams.

Forgiveness, love, listening and communication are the keys to success. I have learned to forgive myself for not being perfect, for not being invincible and for having a condition that makes me feel broken. Forgiveness allows me to see through the haze of shame and guilt revealing the opportunities and resources that abound around me.

I've learned the value of love. Love is acceptance of an individual's strengths and imperfections. In the same way, I have learned how to love myself. I now have a relationship with my condition, embracing all the give-and-take that's involved. I must continuously recognize how it shows up in my life. I must "hear" the revving inside me when I'm approaching mania and address it early. I must listen to its needs so I can adjust my approach accordingly...working *with* it instead of fighting *against* it.

I hope that this handbook can offer you the same support it provided me in building a RELATIONSHIP with myself and others. To begin, I share with you my blog posting:

Why People May Not Get You
http://sharingthejourney.postagon.com/

Today I share an awakening, a context for me to live a successful, meaningful, and desired quality of life while accommodating the needs associated with the volatile and intense emotional experiences (*passion*) of a bipolar condition. That is Albert Mehrabian's 7%-38%-55% rule. Now in the fairness of science, there exist challenges to the exact validity of this rule, but for my personal experience, it has made all the difference I need.

Mehrabian states that there are three elements in face-to-face communication: words (7%), tone of voice (38%), and body language (55%). I then applied my personal experience to this model in the following way: the 7% words include data, information, and "being right." The 38% tone of voice includes emotion, passion, and feelings. The 55% body language includes action.

American society is extremely data-driven, focusing on information and specificity. This means that as the appropriate words and actions for a particular circumstance become more specific and the repercussions of the wrong words and actions become greater. This tightening of appropriate words and actions (7% data) affects the expression of my *passion* (38% emotion) because as the right way becomes more specific, there become more wrong ways to sort through. This leaves me not only stuck with the inability to appropriately share my passion with others, but the guilt of being wrong about the way I tried. In addition, my actions (55% body language) weren't right and were thus abnormal. So what I realized was that it wasn't necessarily that I had moments of intense passion that was the problem, but that the passion wasn't channeled in a healthy, socially acceptable way when I had it.

I'm *not* stating that the *passion* is always pleasurable or easy, because it's not. What I *am* saying is that the inability to channel that *passion* in the right way is a significant source of stress and intensifies the distress of the experience. Developing both a team of people *and* a set of activities that can respect and accommodate the intensity of my *passion* has proven to be a life changer because I no longer need to feel guilty about the swings. I can simply channel them into the appropriate activities to accommodate the needs of the *passion* while pursuing a desired quality of life.

> *Dreams are never destroyed by circumstances. They are born of the heart and of the mind and only there can they ever die. Because while the difficult takes time, the impossible just takes a little longer.*
> —Art E. Berg from the third serving of *Chicken Soup for the Soul*

Living a dream is a dance between the personal growth of an individual and the evolution of an idea. You're going to feel lost, alone, overwhelmed, hollow, nervous, sad, worthless, doubtful, vulnerable, intimidated, lethargic, mentally foggy, and uncomfortable and going to die anyway, regardless of what you do. Why? Because you are human ... an imperfect being requiring skills and tools to accommodate needs and enjoy a desired quality of life.
So ... live ☺
—Stephen Nawotniak

1 Understanding Myself

"Who am I?" This is a fundamental question we all have, and it is a question whose answer changes through time. It has been known throughout the ages that self-awareness is a key to unlocking sources of joy and fulfillment. This question's answer can become blurred under stress and questioned when suffering from symptoms of a chronic condition.

This chapter uses seven activities to help you define yourself as something separate from stressors and medical conditions. It is to help reveal the core principles you wish to build upon and hold true to amid the chaotic storms life can send your way. Be kind to yourself in this section, for it is a sifting process. Don't worry about finding the *right principle* the first time. As you review the information over time, the core principles will continue to resonate, and the more superficial ones will become apparent.

I suggest you follow the *rule of ish*. That is, if it feels right-*ish*, keep it. As you go along, you will notice things have varying levels on your *ishness scale*. Let the principles low on the scale drop off, while you key in on the ones high on the scale.

Activity 1: Self Discovery

Instruction

The purpose of this activity is to gather some information on personality type, learning style and career interests through a variety of means. This awareness provides an important grounding point to help us distinguish "who we are" from the "the condition". These tests frequently uncover aspects of yourself that you "always knew but could never really put into words". It is interesting to see how a variety of test approaches can often lead to the same fundamental results.

Example

When I was diagnosed with bipolar, one of my first questions was "So, who or what am I?" I felt lost because I wasn't sure what was truly me vs. what was coming from the mood disorder during its swings. What was the thing that I couldn't control that kept showing up? What was this beast I felt chasing me, threatening to devour me if I stopped pushing myself? What was this puppeteer that was pulling the strings behind my life? And, most importantly, where am I in all of this? The activities that follow gave me some information I could use to help me distinguish my true self from the one embellished through my symptoms.

Exercise

The links I have included here have been selected because they are free and provide additional directions to pursue if you are interested in their approach. They have been selected from a Google search because they are free and can be accessed through public computers at a library or community centers. Career counselors may also have resources to support this activity.

The links below show a variety of personality tests; some are based on color and some are based on questions that seem irrelevant. The interesting thing is regardless of how the test is developed, you'll see that there are a number of overlaps between the different tests. The information that shows up consistently, regardless of the tests you take, is the information you want to focus on.

Key in on what seems to resonate in you and enjoy the process of self discovery!

Personality Type	Learning Style	Career Fields
ENFP – an "idea" and "people" person. See everyone and everything as part of a whole. Want to help and be liked by people. Great at brainstorming, can have trouble with follow-through.	**Active** – learn by doing **Intuitive** – good at abstract theories **Visual** – remember what I see over what I hear **Global** – learn in large jumps, grasp big picture but may have difficulty explaining how I did it.	Literature and writing Humanities Religious Studies Psychology Counseling

Personality Type
Free Online Personality Tests
http://www.humanmetrics.com/cgi-win/JTypes2.asp
http://www.colorquiz.com/
http://www.personalitytest.net/cgi-bin/q.pl
http://www.learnmyself.com/
http://www.41q.com/
http://www.funeducation.com/Tests/PersonalityTest/TakeTest.aspx
http://www.personalitypathways.com/faces.html
http://www.7personalitytypes.com/
http://www.itstime.com/game.htm
http://changingminds.org/disciplines/storytelling/characters/pearson_archetypes.htm
http://www.capt.org/mbti-assessment/type-descriptions.htm

Learning Style
Free Online Learning Style Assessments
http://managementhelp.org/prsn_dev/lrn_styl.htm
http://www.engr.ncsu.edu/learningstyles/ilsweb.html
http://www.berghuis.co.nz/abiator/lsi/lsiframe.html

Career Fields
Free Online Career Tests
http://www.careerpath.com/
http://www.free-career-test.com/
http://www.careertest.net/index.htm
http://take-a-free-career-test.com/
http://www.careercolleges.com/career-assessment-test.jsp
http://www.ksde.org/Default.aspx?tabid=1801
http://www.rileyguide.com/assess.html

Personality Type	Learning Style	Career Fields

Activity 2: Roles and Personal Mission Statement

Instruction

We have a variety of roles in our lives such as spouse, parent, sibling, child, employee, employer, student, etc. In each role, we have duties and responsibilities that remain constant regardless of our moods. These roles continue as we learn about our condition. The purpose of this activity is to document the type of person we want to be in each of the roles. It provides a reference point, or mission, from which to act while experiencing the volatility of emotion.

Example

My disorder is manifested by rapid cycling. I find that my moods and symptoms can shift fairly quickly. If I focus on my feelings, I find myself a little lost. When I focus on desired actions to fulfill a specific role, I find I have an anchor point to from which to act with meaningful purpose during a time of emotional distress. I also find that when I focus on my individual roles I am able to experience stability. I find it interesting that I can act differently depending on what role I am in. When I'm with my parents, my role of a son is very different than when I am the therapist working with the patient. I also find that each role has different expected behaviors and choices. When I am out with my friends for the evening, there are behaviors that would not be appropriate at work.

In reviewing my various roles, I am primarily grounded in my work role as an Occupational Therapist. My personal mission guides the way I work with my clients during my various mood states. As I work with this activity, I uncover other roles I operate within. This awareness is helpful because when I am feeling stress or difficulty fulfilling one role, I have others to identify success with. This helps provide a sense of balance as difficulty in one role does not ruin my overall self identity and confidence.

Role	Mission
Occupational Therapist	I am a guide and a safe place for my patients to face challenges.
Son	I am a safety net for my parents and their legacy.

Exercise

Now it's your turn. First, list the roles you see yourself in. Then, write a statement of what or who you want to be in each of those roles.

Role	Mission

Activity 3: Dreams, Hopes, Aspirations

Instruction

Life is a constantly changing, growing, developing journey. We have the opportunity to choose our actions in any situation. Those choices can be based on feelings, immediate needs, long term goals, and principles. We often think and talk about things that "would be nice someday." A common tool for success is listing out goals, those things that we wish to achieve. A study by Gail Matthews, Ph.D., Dominican University, showed that people who write down their goals have a higher rate of achievement than people who don't write down their goals. Since a bipolar diagnosis is something that we have, not something that we are, listing out our goals and dreams helps to define ourselves. This section is about the "big picture stuff that would be cool to achieve some day."

Example

My list consists of big picture stuff like traveling around the country, seeing the seven ancient wonders of the world, and being a life coach. It also consists of smaller practical stuff like paying off all my debts. I find that my list changes based on how I feel. When I am hypomanic I have big picture ideas and grandiose concepts. In that moment everything makes sense, anything is doable and it can all be completed quickly and easily. When I am depressed, the same dreams and hopes seem daunting and overwhelming and I have more short-term immediate goals like getting out of bed and getting dressed. I am also quicker to judge my goals/dreams and delete them from the list.

What I have learned is that this is a process of reflection more than an activity to be completed. The nice thing about this list is that during the transition times between my moods, when I feel lost, I have things to start me up again. If I can tick off the short term goals I achieved, I can spend time looking at what I had accomplished versus looking at what I have yet to achieve. Reviewing this list also helps me to separate, in my mind, where I am going versus what mood I am experiencing.

The list gives me something to refer to over time and helps weed out what clicked and what didn't. It also gives me the chance to harness and hold some the creativity and out-of-the-box thinking consistent with a hypomanic state. Big ideas, grandiose ideas, are not necessarily bad. They can often give us a good direction to go in. Regardless of whether or not we complete them, the journey can be very valuable. The key is focusing on developing the steps to get there instead of thinking about whether the goal can be accomplished.

Dreams, Hopes, Aspirations	Supporting Factors	Opposing Factors
Publish this handbook	Personal and professional experience	Writing a self-help book is new
Become debt-free	Have income stream and a plan	Mania can influence spending

Exercise

Relax; you are not creating the "cloud parting enlightening experience" here. You are simply writing down your thoughts, wishes, and interests. As you make this list and reflect upon it, your dreams, hopes and aspirations will start to separate themselves out between superficial interests, meaningful endeavors, and exciting goals. Don't judge, just let the creativity flow. Give yourself permission to dream.

For this activity, you will list your dreams, hopes, and aspirations for yourself and your life. Then list what factors support the reality and what factors don't.

Dreams, Hopes, Aspirations	Supporting Factors	Opposing Factors

Activity 4: Hobbies

Instruction

Wellness is a component of a healthy lifestyle. Work and play are both important activities; work supports and play recharges. Hobbies are the activities that we do to broaden our experiences and enjoy our life. Whether they are working out creating something, developing something or enjoying multiple activities, they give us a variety of tools to work with. Hobbies will be used in the "My Diagnosis" section to help maintain a good quality-of-life while experiencing a mood flare-up. In this activity, it's important to realize that hobbies are part of who we are and what we like to do. Hobbies are associated with our sense of self and are not grounded necessarily in the mood disorder.

Types of Activities

Physical: Focus is on the use of the body to accomplish a task. This can cause physical fatigue (sports, exercise, landscaping/yard work, rock climbing, walking, running, etc.). These activities work large muscle groups and can create an overall body soreness in the following days.

Creative/Intellectual: Focus is on the mind and the manipulation of thoughts (playing an instrument, drawing, writing poetry, planning projects, playing the stock market, learning a language, playing chess/checkers, etc.). These activities can create an expanded awareness and altered perspective, helping us see the world in new ways.

Quiet: These activities are accomplished in a calming environment (meditation, reading, playing solitaire, sunbathing, camping, bird-watching, hunting, watching a movie, etc.). These activities help us let go of life's stresses and constant bombardment of sensory stimuli.

Social: Focus is on activity with people where relationships are created (team sports, card clubs, dancing, etc.). These help us develop our social network and sense of belonging to a community.

Example

I love self-defense and exploring. I enjoy playing my guitar, trying to ballroom dance, and watching movies. Each one of my hobbies has different characteristics. Self-defense is very physical and I find it very grounding because of the sensory input I get from doing it. I find playing the guitar relaxing. The songs I play can help reflect how I feel and help me work through that feeling. The reason I know these are true interests and not interests brought on by the condition is because my interest remains consistent regardless of how I feel. I may not be able to do them the same way or I may not have the energy to do them in the moment, but when I come out of an episode, I still enjoy them.

Physical	Creative/Intellectual	Quiet	Social
Self-defense	Play guitar	Watch movies	Play cards
Dancing	Learn Spanish	Read	Going out for dinner

Exercise

For this activity, list out the things you enjoy doing. This reference list will be utilized in later chapters to help develop a customized plan for balancing a lifestyle and assist with medical management. There are four categories: physical, creative/intellectual, quiet, and social. Each type of category has value and is a key component in a balanced life. Separate your hobbies into the categories they fit into. It is okay if they are in multiple categories.

Now it's your turn:

Physical	Creative/Intellectual	Quiet	Social
_____	_____	_____	_____
_____	_____	_____	_____
_____	_____	_____	_____
_____	_____	_____	_____
_____	_____	_____	_____
_____	_____	_____	_____
_____	_____	_____	_____
_____	_____	_____	_____
_____	_____	_____	_____
_____	_____	_____	_____
_____	_____	_____	_____
_____	_____	_____	_____

Activity 5: Priorities

Instruction

All things do not carry the same priority all the time. The same thing can be more important or less important given the moment. As we better understand our priorities, we choose what actions we take to meet them. Priorities are tied into our principles, our internal sense of value and what's right and wrong. Priorities are influenced by dreams and aspirations and/or goals. Priorities also help us consistently live out our dreams, aspirations and goals. Priorities are the cornerstone of our personality. Episodes may help us reflect on our priorities or help us forget priorities, but episodes are not the source of priorities. Who we are, our sense of self, our identity develops our priorities.

In today's fast-paced society, we are exposed to a tremendous amount of information on a daily basis. With so much media, advertising, and social pressures around it is easy to lose ourselves in superficial activities. It is also easy to have the important things get put on the backburner for apparently more urgent short term needs. It is therefore useful to list the factors that are important and to rank them. The list will change over time. In fact, it should. So what's important to you? As you continue in this process of self reflection and lifestyle development, you may find things that once seemed important fall off your list and new ones take their place. Relax, this all part of the dynamic of self discovery. Also, try to "listen" to the reason WHY these are important for it is the *why* that we want to nurture.

Try not to be judgmental about the reasons for your priorities. What matters is that you identify them. Selfish desires can have a selfless result and quite often, apparently selfless priorities are driven by selfish reasons. Again, these priorities are not determined by the diagnosis, but by who you are. You may find that your priorities are muffled by the symptoms of your diagnosis, but the priorities are driven by your own sense of self. These will be anchors to return to while you're facing uncomfortable situations.

Example

This is a rather difficult exercise for me. For a long time I felt I should be able to be strong all the time and that I should be able to always make the right decision. I should be able to not take things personally and I should be "further along" in my life's journey than I was. This "should" mentality drove me and fed into many upsets because, at the root of all that, I should not be having my episodes. When I started to focus on priorities, it became less of what I "should do" and more about choosing what I "will do" in the moment.

A big priority for me is to successfully live with my bipolar diagnosis so that it will not beat me. For me, this is more important than financial security, more important than comfort, and more important than an image. It is this priority that has led me to Occupational Therapy. It is this priority that has led me to practicing and developing the activities in this book. It was also this priority that has helped me to take that "one extra step" after I felt like giving up.

Being debt free is another priority that I have. I had liberally used my credit card and I realized that everything was costing more because I had to pay interest on what I wanted. I was also seeing my credit cards as available money as opposed to emergency money. The danger of this mindset became incredibly apparent when I was in my depressive episodes because I was not able to generate the same kind of income as when I was in my manic moments.

Debt is a stressor. It has become a consistent prison that I will always be accountable for and calls from creditors can be a huge source of stress. Reading about the "Transforming Debt into Wealth Program" by John Commuta opened my eyes to the process of climbing out of debt. The "Rich Dad, Poor Dad" series by Robert Kiyosaki helped me understand the difference between assets and liabilities.

I find that when climbing out of debt became a clear priority with concrete goals and a concrete plan, I am developing a thought process and system that helps me to challenge manic spending urges. It does not eliminate manic spending urges or the "I need this now" feeling. Setting priorities gives me a choice. When I am standing in line to get to the register or in my car driving home, the time gives me the opportunity to think about what I am buying in comparison to my priorities. I find that I now return items I had purchased more frequently. Time, I learned, is your ally when it comes to clarifying priorities.

Rank	Priority	Reason
1	Successfully living with bipolar disorder	When I am older I want the memories of the experiences I have had and the challenges I have overcome, not excuses or reasons "why not"
2	Being debt-free	I want the freedom to use my money as I want, not "leasing" my lifestyle from my creditors
3	Publish this book	Writing it helps me create a life plan for my own success, people I've shared the idea with feel it can help them as well, and a source of extra income can help me become debt free faster

Exercise

Begin by listing your priorities in the following chart. After that, list out *why* each is important. It is the *why* behind your priority that provides the motivation to persevere though adversity.

Rank	Priority	Reason

Activity 6: Resources

Instruction

Now that we have created some lists of our personal goals, interests, and priorities, start thinking and researching what resources are available to support you in these areas (community clubs for themed activities, Small Business Administration and SCORE for entrepreneurship, adult education programs for special interests, support groups for concerns, etc.). You are not alone in the world and while your life journey and situation may be unique to you, there are many people walking parallel journeys that can help along the way. You will be amazed how much is truly available when you are willing to look and listen.

Remember, the source for problem solving and searching for those resources comes from who we are. This is separate and distinct from a diagnosis and how we feel. It is not about doing everything perfectly all at once. It is about consistently developing that awareness list and performing those actions that make everything possible.

Example

As stated earlier, my first attempt to bounce back after being diagnosed with bipolar disorder was by taking a job with the Boy Scouts of America. Within the year I was nominated for the top district executive award in the Northeast Region. However, that success was based on utilizing my hypomania which I thought I could control without setbacks. The following the year, I crashed. It was then that I realized the manic schedule and demands associated with my job lacked the structure I needed to maintain my own stability.

When I was experiencing myself crashing, I realized I could not do this job. I also realized that I had no idea what I could do. I was frightened. It was then that I started to look at what programs were available for individuals with disabilities, specifically with mental health issues.

I found out about a program in New York State called Vocational and Educational Support for Individuals with Disabilities, VESID for short. VESID provides rehabilitative services "to persons with emotional, mental, or physical disabilities to help them prepare for and obtain gainful employment." After applying and being accepted, I met my counselor, Jack.

Jack was assigned as my VESID counselor and guided me in transforming my attitude toward my bipolar diagnosis from an illness to a relationship based approach. He introduced me to Occupational Therapy, a career that would fulfill my love of teaching and provide me with the structure of an 8 hour day. VESID allowed me to get the assistance needed to determine what kind of job would accommodate the needs of the diagnosis as well as help with funding to support me going back to school.

A second example is unrelated to bipolar disorder, but is related to finding the support that was available when I planned my trek around the country. As mentioned earlier, during the initial planning of the trek, people where skeptical and thought the task seemed too daunting. As I planned out the goals of the project I learned that Buffalo State College would allow me to do a self-designed Masters degree. I found that my involvement with the educational institution gave me the credibility and the prestige of my professors helped to open doors. Suddenly, the trek that had seemed big and unrealistic became credible because it was part of a Masters program. I also found out that AmeriCorps has programs that can help. Based on a proposal I submitted to them, I was able to be an AmeriCorps volunteer while I was doing my trip so I received a stipend, health insurance and an educational award toward my student loans when my service with AmeriCorps was completed.

Item	Resources
Successfully living with bipolar disorder	VESID, counselor, medications
College Degree	College/University, Americorps, scholarships

Exercise

So far in this Section you listed your dreams, hopes and aspirations. You created priorities to help direct your progress towards one of those dreams or aspirations. Now you will list the resources available to support you in these priorities. This is information that will be further developed in the *Structure* Section. For now, let's start thinking about what is available.

Item	Resources

2 Understanding My Condition

Activity 1: Name/Nature of Condition
Activity 2: My Condition's Expression
Activity 3: Medications and Side Effects
Activity 4: Activities
Activity 5: Sensory Integration
Activity 6: Gratitude
Activity 7: Phase-Specific Days
Activity 8: Letters to Self
Activity 9: Resiliency

So you have been given the diagnosis of having bipolar disorder. Have you accepted it or are you still in denial? Accept and even embrace your "disorder" because it is a part of who you are. Remember—you aren't bipolar, you *have* bipolar disorder. This is an essentially important distinction because to say you are bipolar insinuates that that is all you are; to say you have bipolar means that it is just one part of who you are.

Having bipolar disorder is not a death sentence; it does not in *any* way mean that you cannot lead a productive, happy life. It does mean that you face different and more severe challenges throughout your life. It does mean that you will most likely take medication for the rest of your life. This is where many people with bipolar have an issue; however, if you had diabetes or some other disorder, you would also have to take medication every day. Medication, in the grand scheme of things, is not a big deal when compared to the alternatives, which include jail, financial ruin, death, and so on. We will discuss medications later in this chapter.

Acceptance is not easy; this is true. Once you have accepted that you have bipolar, a whole world of options opens up for you. Counseling and medication will be a part of your life, but only one part. One major thing that helped me was researching bipolar. In doing so, I realized just how many famous and influential people had bipolar disorder (Catherine Zeta-Jones, Sting, Congressman Patrick J. Kennedy, and Maurice Benard, to name a few). It's quite amazing how many there are. It made sense to me because our temperaments and qualities lend themselves to being movers and shakers. When I started finding ways in which my bipolar qualities were positive, I truly started healing.

When we have hit the bottom and we are given this diagnosis, there is a mourning period that we go through—mourning a "normal" life that will never be, mourning the losses we have suffered, and dealing with the fallout of our manic and depressive episodes. The intensity of these feelings passes. Life does go on, and you have to be the one to take the reins and make that happen. The best way I have found for living successfully with bipolar is to develop a relationship with our disorder. Learn about it; figure out how it shows up in your life, for it is a part of you.

Activity 1: Name/Nature of Condition

Instruction

Bipolar disorder is very individualized and can affect people in a variety of ways. My friends and I have experienced times that are similar to those who suffer with ADHD (attention deficit/hyperactivity disorder), OCD (obsessive compulsive disorder), and high anxiety. It is easy to become overwhelmed with all these terms. Remember, a diagnosis is a group of symptoms that are given a name. It does not define you. As we understand the different ways that the diagnosis shows up, we can begin to understand how it personally affects our lives. This takes it from being a list on a page or a name in a book to having a personal impact.

Diagnosis

Type I: Have a single manic or hypomanic episode and no past major depressive episodes.
Type II: Have at least one hypomanic episode and one depressed episode.
Rapid Cycle: Four or more episodes in a single year.
Mixed: Meet the requirements for both a manic and depressive episode at the same time for a week.

Symptom Description

Mania: Three or more of the following symptoms lasting a week: inflated self-esteem/grandiosity; decreased need for sleep (fine after 3 hours); more talkative than normal/pressed to keep talking; flight of ideas/racing thoughts; distractibility; increase in psychomotor activity/goal-directed activity; excessive involvement in high-risk activities.

Hypomania: Three or more of the following symptoms lasting at least four days: inflated self-esteem/grandiosity; decreased need for sleep (fine after 3 hours); more talkative than normal/pressed to keep talking; flight of ideas/racing thoughts; distractibility; increase in psychomotor activity/goal-directed activity; excessive involvement in high-risk activities

Depression: Five or more of the following symptoms over two weeks: depressed mood most of the day; diminished pleasure/interest in daily activities; significant weight loss when not dieting; insomnia/hypersomnia; psychomotor agitation or retardation nearly every day; fatigue or energy loss; feelings of worthlessness or inappropriate guilt; diminished ability to think clearly.

Example

I have a bipolar II, rapid cycling with mixed states diagnosis. Before medication and counseling I had spikes in my emotions where I had a couple of days of very high-energy creativity and enthusiasm, where I am incredibly productive and very creative. I fell in love with these high times and began to identify them as "who I was" or my "normal". But what goes up must come down. I would have crashes that lasted a couple of days to a couple of weeks. This up-and-down experience identified itself as what was normal for me. What I didn't understand, however, was that it was not normal for the majority of the population. As I talked with other individuals who also have a bipolar diagnosis, I realized that the diagnosis shows up uniquely in each person's life. Some people can have a manic episode that goes on for weeks where they only sleep a couple of hours per night and are able to keep going. Others can have months in the depressed episode and periodically have intermittent high times. Mine is one of instability and constant change.

My Type	Description
Type II, Rapid Cycle, Mixed	I can get short periods of hypomania, mania, and depression. They typically last from a couple of days to a couple of months and one symptom is frequently followed by another. I can also have periods with the restlessness and racing thoughts of mania with the hollowness and fatigue of depression.

Exercise

Take this time to identify some of the characteristics you are experiencing with your disorder. In the chart below, list out your types and a description of *how* you experience them in *your* life.

While this does not replace a diagnosis of a trained professional, this can help you provide a trained professional with information to assist in making an accurate diagnosis.

My Type	Description

Activity 2: My Condition's Expression

Instruction

It is important that we uncover the various components of our condition's expression. By understanding how it shows up and what its needs are, we can better accommodate those needs while moving toward our goals in life. Ultimately, we can live a life of quality in a meaningful relationship with the diagnosis.

Example

When I first found out about my condition, I viewed it as something to control or something to manage. I was used to acute short-term illnesses that I could fix or work my way through, like a cold or the flu. Over the course of the first few months after diagnosis, I found, for the first time in my life, I was face-to-face with something that I could not simply will myself through.

As I spent time writing down my physical feelings, thoughts, emotions, actions, triggers, benefits, and dangers, I began to understand what my condition's needs were. I began to understand the things that I had to accommodate, and what I had to take into account in order to live out my life. For instance, with my mania I would try to do everything all at once. By creating a chart I could see that while I would have great ideas, I would not have a foundation that could sustain those ideas. From a depression point of view, I realized that during the time before and after a depressive episode, I was more sensitive to the needs of others. It gave me empathy. It gave me the chance to understand that pain and turmoil have universal components regardless of the actual situation causing them. As I began to understand and work with my pain, it taught me the skills necessary to help others through their pain.

Looking at the condition as an entity to understand, instead of an illness to beat, allowed me to create a relationship with it. I no longer focused on trying to recover from being sick, but what I could be learning from my current situation. I now focus on getting to know the different characteristics, needs, and opportunities associated with the diagnosis and reflect on the condition's expression within me.

Below is the chart I have created over time as I have developed a relationship with my own diagnosis. You are free to use it as a reference point for your own and you may find many parts the same, but remember it is about creating a relationship, not just listing facts.

My Condition's Expression

Stage	Physical Feelings	Thoughts	Emotions	Actions	Triggers	Benefits	Dangers
Manic	Racing heart, light-headed	Racing thoughts, unable to focus, want to do everything at once	Anger, excitement	Jump from project to project without completing one	Feeling overwhelmed, riding hypomania without discretion	Chance to separate self from feelings for a more self-generated life	Inappropriate actions, $ problems, damage relationships
Hypo-manic	Energized motivated, fidgety	Creative, quicker with what I can do, single-minded, self-absorbed	Hope, inspiration	Take on large projects, start additional projects	Challenge	Heightened productivity	Take on too much, turn into mania
Anxiety	Acidic stomach, feel like I'm crawling out of my skin, fidgetiness	Something is going to fall apart on me, doubt people's authenticity	Nervous	Review plans	New situations, getting close to someone, having good things last	Places emphasis on the systems put in place	Self-sabotage my situation
Bummed	Tired, minor illness, anxiety	Slower, foggy	Sad, scared, intimidated	Increasingly ask people for help on projects, back down from projects	Crash from mania	More sensitive to another's feelings, introspective, more objective with decisions	Become too clingy, full of depression
Depressed	Heavy, exhausted, empty	Hopeless, numbness, fogginess	Emptiness, loneliness	Sleep, withdraw	Overwhelmed, important loss	Chance to separate self from feelings for a more self-generated life	Personal injury, social isolation, ignore responsibility

Exercise

Spend time reflecting on the condition's unique expression of itself in your own life. While there are clinical lists of potential symptoms, the important piece to focus on is the unique, personal expression in your life. As you identify them and fill out this chart, you will become better at identifying the characteristics, recognizing an episode, and making proactive choices to address the episode's needs. Awareness is the first step in this process, and the following chart helps to create that awareness.

Stage	Physical Feelings	Thoughts	Emotions	Actions	Triggers	Benefits	Dangers

Activity 3: Medications and Side Effects

Instruction

Medication is used to shorten peaks and valleys to a livable level, not to eliminate symptoms. It is important to remember that everybody's chemistry is different and that the dosage is related to your body's processing of the chemical. Also, doctor supervision and regular blood tests are required to monitor the drugs' effects. The following chart was developed from the information found within *The Merck Manual, 18th edition* (Merck Research Laboratories, 2006 Whitehouse Station, NJ).

Drug Category	Effect	Possible Side Effects
(SSRIs) Selective serotonin reuptake inhibitors	Keep serotonin (a chemical responsible for supporting brain activity) high by preventing it from being absorbed back into the body	Increased agitation for first couple of weeks; possible increase of suicidal thoughts and attempts in adolescents and children in first few months; changes in bowel movements
Serotonin modulators	Similar to SSRIs but work on 5-HT (a slightly different chemical) by preventing it from being absorbed back into the body	Can damage liver; fatigue; affect weight
Serotonin-norepinephrine reuptake inhibitors	Keep serotonin and norepinephrine (two chemicals responsible for supporting brain activity) high by preventing them from being absorbed back into the body	Nausea during first 2 weeks; irritability, anxiety, nausea if stopped suddenly
Dopamine-norepinephrine reuptake inhibitors	Keep dopamine and norepinephrine (two chemicals responsible for supporting brain activity) high by preventing them from being absorbed back into the body	Hypertension; agitation; reversible memory loss if overmedicated

Drug Category	Effect	Possible Side Effects
Heterocyclic antidepressants	Prevent norepinephrine and 5-HT (two chemicals responsible for supporting brain activity) high by preventing them from being absorbed back into the body	Toxicity with high levels; constipation
MAOIs	Prevent breakdown of norepinephrine, dopamine, or 5-HT	Can cause harmful reactions with certain foods; erectile dysfunction; anxiety; nausea; dizziness; insomnia; weight gain

Example

Before I was taking meds, I identified who I was and where I wanted to be with the energy, creativity, and euphoria of the hypomanic state. When I wasn't in that state, I was pushing myself to get there because that's where I was most effective. That's where I made the most progress and felt most alive. When I was growing up and into my early twenties, the benefits of the hypomania outweighed the negatives of the crash that followed. But then, the crashes became debilitating. What I had to understand was the difference between long-term benefits versus short-term gains. I had to acknowledge the fact that while the hypomania would help me get ten steps forward, the crash would set me fifteen steps back. So in the process of letting go of the hypomanic state, I had to let go of my desired norm. It became a grieving process, a sense of loss.

I find that the medications help temper my highs and lows so they were more manageable, but they do not eliminate them. I also find that sometimes my creativity is stifled. What I used to be able to crank out in three days when I was in a hypomanic state can now take longer and require additional assistance from others. The most important effect of medication is sustainability. By that I mean I can now continue to steadily build on what I am accomplishing, instead of overwhelming myself with too many projects.

As odd as this may sound, I now identify myself now with the slightly down state. I find that I listen better, have more empathy, and am more grounded. I now know the difference between the feelings of fulfillment from experiencing long-term success versus the excitement of a short-term high. I don't see the depression as all bad anymore. I now see it as a normal part of being human, just like excitement and joy. For me the process of accepting the medication involved letting go of who I thought I needed to be in order to accept a new state of being. The frustration in the beginning was that I felt I was losing what I loved most about myself while gaining a bunch of negative side effects. I now see that my premedication identity consisted of unrealistic expectations that set me up for failure. While I do miss my hypomanic highs and creativity, I am finding I get to enjoy a lot more now with my new sense of identity, more realistic expectations, and greater empathy for others.

Just as my diagnosis doesn't have *every* listed symptom, I do not experience every potential side effect from my medication. Also, by understanding the negative side effects, I can plan activities to help address them. Understanding the *why* of the medication helps to validate its necessity when I get frustrated about the loss of my hypomanic freedom. Finally, when the negative aspect of the side effect outweighs the benefit of the drug, I have something specific to talk to my doctor/psychiatrist about. Below is a chart on a couple of the medications I tried.

Medication	Effect	Why Take?	Dose	Time	Side Effects	Counter-action
Depakote	Mood stabilizer	Balance moods	20mg	Night	Weight gain; can't think clearly	Exercise one hr. per day; take notes.
Celexa	Antide-pressant	Keep from suicidal thoughts	40mg	2x daily, night and morning	Toxicity	Monitor blood levels.

Exercise

Now that you have a broad sense of the categories used, list the information about your own specific medications and how they affect you.

Medication	Effect	Why Take?	Dose	Time	Side Effects	Counteraction

Activity 4: Activities

Instruction

As we look at our lifestyles and understand our triggers, we can identify activities of interest that can have a regulating effect on our current symptoms. In general, active activities can help to counter a depressed mood and calming activities can help to ground a manic mood.

Activities are a key component in quality of life. When I was first diagnosed, I felt like I had to focus on getting well before I could do things that I wanted to do. It is important to understand the nature of the condition and create a relationship with it before major decisions are made, life doesn't wait for you to feel good. It took me some time, but I've learned that the kind of activities I do can make a difference in how I feel.

Just as activities have various steps to be successful, there are various characteristics of an activity that can affect a person. I give you the example of drinking a cup of warm herbal tea. From a sensory point of view, you feel the weight of the cup, the heat of the water, and the smell and taste of the tea. Teas can have various nutritional qualities, such as energy from caffeine, health properties from green tea, and relaxation qualities from certain herbal blends.

Because tea has various characteristics, the activity can be used to satisfy a variety of needs. Caffeinated tea can be drunk to energize a person when tired. Noncaffeinated herbal teas can be drunk to help settle an upset stomach or help a person relax before bed. A hot tea can help warm a person up in winter. A cold tea can help refresh a person in summer. So the varying qualities and characteristics of an activity can be used to address an individual's needs in a given situation. Also, an activity can be slightly modified to better meet the demands of a specific situation.

In relation to mood disorder, activities can be used to address and compensate for the unique demands of different mood episodes. Some characteristics of each episode and examples of activities that can support a desired quality of life during them are as follows:

Depressed—exhaustion, poor problem-solving ability, poor attention, negative thoughts, difficulty with detail work. The kinds of activities that are beneficial during this episode have the following characteristics: familiar, big movement, medium weight, comforting, draw attention away from thinking into expressing or doing, easily successful. The key of these activities is to get out of your own head.

Down—low energy, decreased problem-solving ability, moderately withdrawn, increased empathy. The kinds of activities that are beneficial during this episode have the following characteristics: service to others, exercise, creativity, moderate challenge. The key of these activities is to help pick up or elevate mood.

Balanced—balanced is not about a happy or sad emotion. Rather, it is the presence of well-regulated energy levels. Any and all activities can be effective.

Hypomania—high energy, increased distractibility, increased creativity, increased risk taking, increased agitation, increased impatience. The kinds of activities that are beneficial during this episode have the following characteristics: heavy work, energy releasers, grounding, provide a creative outlet.

Mania—uncontrolled energy, grandiosity, racing thoughts, risk taking, easily distracted, poor focus and attention span. The kinds of activities that are beneficial during this episode have the following characteristics: running, biking, weeding, cleaning.

Example

When I recognize that I am experiencing the physical sensations, thoughts, and behaviors associated with a *hypomania* episode starting to spiral out of control, I like to go into a darkened room to listen to calming music and focus on breath control. I find that this can help slow my heart rate, relax my emotional rev, and make me aware of my current physiological state. I then have some space to choose actions based on my role-specific mission statement versus how I feel and to provide me the opportunity to be more objective.

When I am experiencing the physical sensations, thoughts, and behaviors associated with a *depressive* episode, I like to write posts for my blog at http://sharingthejourney.postagon. com/. This gives me a channel to convey the emptiness and haunting pain that tend to settle in the center of my chest. I find that when I can put together a set of words that can reflect back to me how I feel, it acts like a pressure-release valve for the aching. I then have access to the experience of positive feedback from people who can relate, reducing the loneliness that so often accompanies the episode.

I have listed out some possible activities in the table on the following page.

Depressed Get out of your head	Down Pickups	Balanced Any	Hypomania Grounding, calming	Mania Release energy
Painting	Volunteering		Tai-chi	Walking/hiking
Poetry	Walking		Yoga	Running
Drawing	Biking		Take a warm shower	Stationary bike
Listening to some inspirational music	Poetry		Listen to quiet music in a dim room	Cleaning
Go out to a movie	Drawing		Get a spa treatment	Weeding
Support group	Support group		Support group	Support group

Exercise

Create a list of activities that you could do in each stage based on what you enjoy doing.

Depressed Get out of your head	Down Pickups	Balanced Any	Hypomania Grounding, calming	Mania Release energy

Activity 5: Sensory Input

Instruction

This section is based on personal experience and professional judgment/reasoning. Bipolar disorder stems from emotional extremes caused by an imbalance of the chemicals in the brain and recent studies point to a relationship with the vagal nerve of the parasympathetic nervous system. There is a physiological basis for our disorder so it makes sense to address the physical needs associated with activating and influencing our nervous system. We interact with our outside environment through our senses and our interpretation of the sensory input we receive can influence our physiological state (fight-or-flight response from apparent danger, relaxation from chamomile or lilac scents, etc.).

Sensory stimulation is used by many Occupational Therapists to make a positive difference in children with self-regulation. Jean Ayres, recognized as a pioneer in this work, has developed this into the Sensory Integration (SI) approach. Many preschool and early intervention programs utilize sensory rooms and weighted objects to help a child improve attention and behavior. Sensory input is also used for individuals with dementia to decrease agitation. We instinctively put on calming music in a darkened setting with scented candles for a relaxed atmosphere. Planned input through our senses can be used to massage our central nervous system and improve self-regulation. There are also multiple books on the use of sensory input with children that are available online, at bookstores, or in your library.

Example

As a traveling therapist, I need to be able to have systems in place that help me function with changes in my emotional state without disrupting my responsibilities. I have found this sensory integration approach to be a very valuable tool. Earlier, I went over the expression of my condition and how it uniquely shows up in my life. Having done that exercise allows me to more effectively recognize when I am entering an episode.

I have learned that when I'm in my depressive episode, I need to be kind to myself. I pick something that tastes good, feels good, smells good, and looks good. All in all, I try to do things that are pleasing and refreshing to the senses. I have noticed that as I do that, I feel calmer and more relaxed, allowing things to balance back.

When approaching mania, I find a similar approach helpful, but my focus is on smell and sound. I find physical activities help with burning off energy, but wearing a compression shirt or a heavy coat/blanket, or holding a soft and weighted object can help ground me and slow down the fidgety side of the hypomania.

This sensory based approach does not take away the episode, but rather gives me a way to ride out the process. It is a conscientious approach to provide soothing stimuli to help me massage and calm my aggravated nervous system.

The table below has some examples of items or activities that I have found pleasant for each sense. As you create your own sensory bag of tricks, you can prepare to have items readily available to use when you feel an episode approaching.

Sight	Sound	Smell	Taste	Touch	Proprioception
Fish tank, lava lamp	Classical music, nature sounds	Smell is a *very* primitive sense, with a short path to the brain. Lilac and vanilla are calming scents.	Choose a couple of favorite flavors.	a fuzzy or fleece blanket, gentle breeze, comfortable temperature. A large section of the brain is dedicated to the sensory input and movements of the hand. Self-massage of the hands helps me when I find a funk coming on.	Awareness of your body's position. Heavy work is grounding. Yoga's Sun Salutation helps to release endorphins and is grounding. Tight Under Armour-style shirt can be grounding.

Exercise

Create a list of some of your own preferred sensory experiences that help you temper the episode experience and pass through it more comfortably. This is not about eliminating the episodes.

Sight	Sound	Smell	Taste	Touch	Proprioception
_____	_____	_____	_____	_____	_____
_____	_____	_____	_____	_____	_____
_____	_____	_____	_____	_____	_____
_____	_____	_____	_____	_____	_____
_____	_____	_____	_____	_____	_____
_____	_____	_____	_____	_____	_____
_____	_____	_____	_____	_____	_____
_____	_____	_____	_____	_____	_____
_____	_____	_____	_____	_____	_____
_____	_____	_____	_____	_____	_____
_____	_____	_____	_____	_____	_____
_____	_____	_____	_____	_____	_____
_____	_____	_____	_____	_____	_____
_____	_____	_____	_____	_____	_____
_____	_____	_____	_____	_____	_____
_____	_____	_____	_____	_____	_____
_____	_____	_____	_____	_____	_____
_____	_____	_____	_____	_____	_____
_____	_____	_____	_____	_____	_____
_____	_____	_____	_____	_____	_____
_____	_____	_____	_____	_____	_____

Activity 6: Gratitude

Instruction

In addition to the psychological perspective our attitudes provide, we have a physiological and chemical response to stimuli and our interpretation of it. If we act as though things are against us, our bodies' activate its fight-or-flight defensive response system. We release chemicals such as adrenaline and we are geared for adversity. When we are present to gratitude, we are more present to abundance and safety. Chemically, our bodies relax, giving us a chance to heal and recharge. We also have the opportunity to see and notice the things we are grateful for. When we conscientiously choose to construct a list, it gives us something to choose to notice.

Example

There are *many* things we can find that we appreciate when we allow ourselves to be present to thankfulness. Gratitude does *not* mean everything is okay. It brings into focus some positive thoughts to help balance the storm of negativity raging in our heads during a depressive episode. As we focus on thankfulness, we begin to become aware and present to what we have in abundance to *give,* instead of what we need. Gratitude and a feeling of abundance provide a nice context from which to live.

For me, it's easy to get lost in my head when I'm in a manic or depressive state. My feelings and emotions take center stage, and it's easy for me to identify with them. I notice that it's easy to focus on things that support or feed into my negative feelings when I'm feeling down and to focus on things that validate possibilities when I'm feeling hypomanic.

I have noticed that the more I try *not* to think about something, the more focused I become on very thing that I am trying to avoid. But if I give my mind a conscious choice, I am better able to focus on one thought at a time. This is the way the Thankful ABCs exercise works. It gives me a format to think of things that I am grateful for and things that bring me joy. The following exercise gives me something to anchor to in either state and helps draw me back to my values and principles. Our minds cannot think of two things at the same time.

A … apples, apple pie, apple pie with vanilla ice cream, yum!
B … my brothers, how we always support each other and mess around when we are together.
C … cats, how it feels good when they are curled up in my lap.

D … dogs, Morgan was my first dog and he was so cool to grow up with.

E … elephants, I don't know why but it popped in my head doing this. I think the long trunk for a nose is cool.

… and so on down the alphabet. As you can see, serious or shallow, the point is to start thinking of positive things—no matter how small or insignificant they may seem.

Exercise

Focus on thankfulness for what you currently have or enjoy. The Thankful ABCs is a good tool to introduce thankfulness and choice to the mind when the destructive thoughts of an episode are running out of control. Think small. As in my personal example, mine often seem to begin with "A … for apples … apple pie."

A. _____

B. _____

C. _____

D. _____

E. _____

F. _____

G. _____

H. _____

I. _____

J. _____

K. _____

L. _____

M. _____

N. _____

O. _____

P. _____

Q. _____

R. _____

S. _____

T. _____

U. _____

V. _____

W. _____

X. _____

Y. _____

Z. _____

Activity 7: Phase-Specific Days

Instruction

Disorders are disorders because they affect our quality of life in a negative way. Just because you feel down doesn't mean you're depressed. Just because you're hopeful and excited doesn't mean you're manic. So part of understanding how our condition manifests itself is also understanding how to address it when it shows up. The challenge here is that the very organ for problem solving, our brain, is the organ that is affected. This means that the ability to critically think and work through a problem objectively is affected when experiencing an episodic flare-up. The goal here is to create templates for when we have our exacerbations, an autopilot to complete meaningful tasks and experience some personal competence on days that our mind just doesn't seem to work quite right.

As you begin to understand yourself, the personality of your disorder, and your current roles/missions, you can preplan some phase-specific days. To address depression, it can be helpful to plan a day of concrete, familiar activities (laundry, dishes, shower, dress, etc.) with the goal of accomplishing one per hour, even use an alarm clock if needed. The focus is "How do I live into my role missions *while* experiencing depression?" To address mania, it can be helpful to list out the heavy jobs that don't require a lot of focus and detail work. Push mowing the lawn, vacuuming *under* the furniture, working a garden or landscaping, and cleaning out the inside of the car are all examples of activities that can burn energy and not necessarily require a lot of detailed thought.

Example

I find that when I have my down days, I have to hold off on major decisions and focus on familiar activities. I use sensory activities interspersed throughout the day to give me breaks. I have a list of familiar things to go through that don't involve a lot of extra thought. I even have it set up to where I have one item to complete per hour. When I am hypomanic, I find that there are so many possibilities and so much to do that I can lose track of where to start. I try to hold off on spending decisions (or at least keep my receipts) and try to focus on big movement/energy projects (laundry, cleaning the garage, mowing the lawn) that I can do while the mind is racing. There is freedom in knowing that I have things planned out in case things go bad. This, I find, helps relieve some of the stress of trying to stay well. Again, the focus of this approach is to live a meaningful quality of life *with* and *during* bipolar episodes.

Depressed	Manic
Go from bed to couch.	Cut grass.
Take shower and get dressed.	Dust furniture.
Shave.	Vacuum rugs under furniture.
Make breakfast.	Do laundry.
Start a load of laundry.	Organize basement.
Wash dishes.	Clean garage.

Exercise

In the chart below, list some activities that could support constructive and meaningful action within each episode. Make this list based on your own lifestyle and interests.

Activity 8: Letters to Self

Instruction

Talk therapy is often used as a complementary treatment method with medicine. It can be helpful to share our experiences in a way that another person can relate and reflect back what we are saying. Writing letters to ourselves can also be helpful. This can help validate our goals and missions and remind us of what we are grateful for. Reading these will allow us to revisit these through our own words, with our own priorities. This can help us work through our emotions and to settle out some of our feelings. We know what we're thinking and a personal letter cuts through the statement, "Well, you don't understand what I'm really feeling." when a well intentioned person is trying to help but doesn't seem to relate.

Example

I find self reflection and writing about my thoughts and feelings helpful. Here is an example of one of my letters for use during my depressive episodes:

> *Steve, I know you are feeling down and that you are in a dark and stormy place, where you don't see a way out and you feel completely alone. The fatigue, the pain, the emptiness can be haunting. This is me talking to you, a lighthouse to help illuminate the way in the darkness and the storm. Remember that this is temporary even though it feels permanent. It's about riding it out and being kind to yourself during the process. You have your sensory things to do, Thankful ABCs to say, and your list of people already in place to talk to if you need it. You have a plan that you can use when you need to, and you are not alone. Remember, courage and quality of life are not passive experiences you receive. They are caused by actively making a living out of choices during times of adversity. This episode is a teacher, helping you to develop important skills, as long as you're willing to learn. Also, there is a unique feeling available: the experience that what you say and do makes a difference, that you make a positive impact on those around you, and you are able to persevere toward things of importance while experiencing discomfort. There is a pride available when you know you can do things while feeling down. Listen; be kind to yourself and recharge. As you read in The Secret, the most important question an individual can ask himself or herself is whether or not the universe is a kind universe. This is not about fair. Things just are what they are. But you get to choose who you will be with them. So relax. You don't have to be 100% right now. You just have to be. Know you're not alone and we will go through this together, step-by-step.*

Exercise

Now, go ahead and write yourself a letter. This is for you to be your own cheerleader, your own voice of reason and no one else needs to read your letter.

_____

_____

_____

_____

_____

_____

_____

_____

_____

_____

_____

_____

Activity 9: Resiliency

Instruction

Resiliency is the ability to recover from major setbacks or disappointments and can apply to mood disorder when we recover from one of our episodic states. Resiliency is a specific life skill that can be learned, developed, and strengthened. According to Al Siebert in his book *The Resiliency Advantage*, resiliency is made up of self-confidence, self-esteem, and self-concept. The important thing is that we understand that it is developed by motivations *within* ourselves and we *have control* over its outcome.

Optimism during depression requires the awareness and belief that we can influence our quality of life through our own conscious choices and actions. Optimism is a skill; depression is a state. We can perform a variety of skills in a variety of states.

Example

For me, the importance of resiliency is most noticeable whenever I come out of my depressions. It is a time when I find myself wondering *What am I doing?* and *What's important to me?* I find that every time I come up from a depressive state or down from a hypomanic state, I feel that things are different and will never go back to how they were before the episode. Now use this state of uncertainty to return to internal principles, review my goals and values, reflect on where my life is now, and choose how to try and live out those principles into the current context or situation.

I find that the consistent change of my moods provides a consistent opportunity for starting over. My first response is always one of frustration. It seems unfair to always have to rebuild my identity after emotional experiences I cannot control. Once again, my diagnosis is my teacher. My emotional roller coaster is a continuous training ground for the skill of consciously *creating* an outlook of opportunity and hope during a state of despair.

I live by the perspective that I can't always control what I am feeling or what happens to me, but I *always* have the choice of how I will react/respond to it. This is a critical belief I have, a cornerstone I start from. It is simply a core belief I have chosen and is independent from how I feel.

What I Am Experiencing	What I Want to Achieve	One Action I Can Take
Being lost, feeling alone, having no direction	To feel connected to someone	Call and help a friend.
Embarrassment, feeling stupid, feeling like a failure	To have something I am proud of	Work on one activity in this book.

Exercise

List the various physical, mental and emotional aspects of the feelings you are experiencing. Then, list what you want different and identify one action you can take to move one step closer toward what you want.

What I Am Experiencing	What I Want to Achieve	One Action I Can Take

3 Creating the Structure

We exist within two worlds: the world we live within and the world that lives within us.

The world we live within consists of our environment, family, and friends. It is where we work, where we play, and where we live. It consists of the rules we must follow, the external stimuli that affect us, and the physical resources we have to draw upon.

The world within us consists of our emotions, perspectives, goals, and values. It is what we believe, how we think, and who we choose to be. It consists of internal stimuli that affect us and the place from which we live.

Both of these worlds can be in a state of order and a state of chaos. These two worlds with two available states provide for potential experiences illustrated by the diagram below.

The Four Quadrants

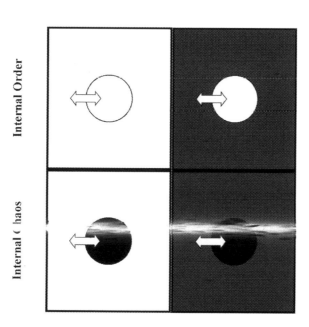

The upper left corner is the ideal win-win situation. It is the state where the environment we live in has order, clear opportunities and resources, and minimal negative stressors. It is also the state where we internally have emotional balance, a clear sense of direction, and a positive mental attitude.

The lower right corner is a lose-lose situation, and unfortunately, the situation in which individuals with mental health or emotional disorders all too often have to live in. It is the state where the environment we live in has high amounts of stress, personal and financial affairs are in disarray, and unexpected demands are constantly placed upon us. It is also the state where we internally are experiencing an episodic flare-up of our mood disorder. We can see that in this situation, successful living is near impossible; life is unfortunately a downward spiral.

The top left corner represents a balanced life and the bottom right corner represents defeat. The middle two corners illustrate how the internal and external worlds can influence each other.

The bottom left corner is a representation of resiliency. Here an individual is remaining calm during a chaotic event or within a chaotic environment. This calm internal state then supports the individual in successfully navigating the challenges of external chaos.

When we look in the top right corner, we have the environment structured and the internal state of the individual chaotic. This is the quadrant that this chapter is all about. It is about creating an external structure to support an individual in completing meaningful activities toward a desired outcome during a chaotic internal state.

Activity 1: Time Log

Instruction

With a mood disorder, our internal feelings and emotions and energy levels can shift. A daily structure gives us something to believe in during a bipolar episode so that we can continue to make small steps toward a desired goal. As we discussed earlier, we have roles and missions and having structure supports us in living out those roles and missions during times when we feel like giving up.

We can also incorporate many common personal-effectiveness programs. Franklin Covey Day Planners, Stephen Covey's *7 Habits of Highly Effective People*, and David Allen's *Getting Things Done* are examples of popular personal-effectiveness programs that business executives implement for themselves. What we will be doing is taking these principles and implementing them in our own lives while accommodating the particular demands of the mood episode we need to accommodate during the day.

Example

I find that the rapid cycling nature of my bipolar disorder makes my expected day-to-day feelings unknown to me. I can wake up each day in a different mood: sometimes excited, sometimes down. Some days I have a burst of creativity and energy; other days I am slow in just getting started. An example is the writing of this book. Quite often some of this was written while sitting down and jotting down some thoughts. Sometimes it took fifteen minutes, sometimes five. I have to structure my day so that I spend some part of everyday typing something on the page (structured time for writing resulted in this handbook).

I find I need to consider the effect of medications on my day. As an occupational therapist I know that it is important to structure the day or organize the environment to support work that needs to be done within the different states I am experiencing. When I find myself with a medication hangover in the morning, I do not try to balance my checkbook. While I was in the process of determining what medication combination and dosage worked best for me, I would have some that left me groggy and drowsy in the morning. During those groggy times, I did not have the intellectual/cognitive/problem-solving ability needed for a detail based activity. Instead, I focus on general movement physical activities like laundry, washing dishes, and cleaning. These activities would help pull me through the mental grogginess. If you find yourself in a consistent medication hangover in the morning, then perhaps a work environment that has a second-shift position or schedule would be beneficial. The key is to understand how things show up in your life so that you can do the right kinds of activities at the right times. Below is the original chart I constructed for myself.

Time	State	Activities
7:00 a.m.	Wake up	Wake up
7:30 a.m.	↑	
8:00 a.m.	**Medication**	Breakfast, shower,
8:30 a.m.	**hangover**	walk, clean, laundry
9:00 a.m.	(low-thinking activities)	
9:30 a.m.	↓	
10:00 a.m.	↑	
10:30 a.m.		Bills, organize, work on project
11:00 a.m.	**Most alert**	
11:30 a.m.	(important activities)	
12:00 p.m.	↓	
12:30 p.m.		Lunch
1:00 p.m.		
1:30 p.m.	↑	
2:00 p.m.	**Tired**	Do laundry, read for pleasure
2:30 p.m.	(easy activities)	
3:00 p.m.	↓	
3:30 p.m.	↑	
4:00 p.m.	**Second wind**	Plan next day, homework,
4:30 p.m.	(next-important activities)	
5:00 p.m.		
5:30 p.m.		Cook
6:00 p.m.	↓	Eat Dinner
6:30 p.m.	↑	Eat
7:00 p.m.	**Tired**	Listen to music, watch TV
7:30 p.m.	(leisure activities)	
8:00 p.m.	↓	
8:30 p.m.	Exhausted	Sleep

Exercise

For this exercise, take time to map out how you feel and what activities you typically do at certain times of the day. Focus on becoming aware of how you feel throughout the day as you perform your routine. This activity provides the basis for time management.

Time	State	Activities
5:00 a.m.		
5:30 a.m.		
6:00 a.m.		
6:30 a.m.		
7:00 a.m.		
7:30 a.m.		
8:00 a.m.		
8:30 a.m.		
9:00 a.m.		
9:30 a.m.		
10:00 a.m.		
10:30 a.m.		
11:00 a.m.		
11:30 a.m.		
12:00 p.m.		
12:30 p.m.		
1:00 p.m.		
1:30 p.m.		
2:00 p.m.		
2:30 p.m.		
3:00 p.m.		
3:30 p.m.		
4:00 p.m.		
4:30 p.m.		
5:00 p.m.		
5:30 p.m.		

Time	State	Activities
6:00 p.m.		
6:30 p.m.		
7:00 p.m.		
7:30 p.m.		
8:00 p.m.		
8:30 p.m.		
9:00 p.m.		
9:30 p.m.		
10:00 p.m.		
10:30 p.m.		
11:00 p.m.		
11:30 p.m.		

Activity 4: Goals

Instruction

Goals are specific tangible accomplishments. Dreams are someday, maybe, would be nice. We will build on this in chapter 3 to help map out a specific plan and integrate the goal and dream into your daily life. For now, we want to just start the process.

Example

The difference between a goal and a dream is not east to uncover. When I am manic or hypomanic, I try to make every dream or hope into a goal. Then when I come down out of a high I have so much going on, so many balls in the air, I can't keep them going and wind up crashing. What I am learning is that it's okay to have a big list of dreams and hopes, but then only pick a couple to work on as official goals. This helps to prioritize things and gives me the freedom for my manic and hypomanic creativity to be an asset instead of being a trap.

A dream of mine is to help improve our understanding of the bipolar condition so it is not such a debilitating experience. My current goal to support this dream is to write this handbook. This goal is tangible because, when the book is published, the goal is met. This goal can be intimidating at times because I am committed to expressing a personal part of myself to others. I have doubts about whether or not this was worthy to share. I question if there is merit to this perspective and whether or not I am actually good enough to enjoy success. As a dream, I can talk about how nice it would be to do. As a goal, I am taking specific actions to accomplish the task.

Priority	Goal	What You Will Do	What You Need
3	Get a job	Write a résumé, send to 5 potential employers	Resume example and a computer
2	Find a counselor I like	Schedule three appointments	Three names, contact numbers, a calendar, and a phone
4	Graduate from college	Apply to five colleges	Five college applications
1	Clean house	Clean bathroom	Cleaning supplies

Exercise

Now it's your turn to list out your goals, one specific step toward the goal and what you need to accomplish the task. Prioritize them according to their level of importance.

Priority	Goal	What You Will Do	What You Need

Activity 3: Milestones

Instruction

Every goal needs to be broken down into a series of smaller steps called milestones. Mapping these steps out is helpful because it gives us direction in attaining our goals. Setting milestones additionally benefits individuals with a mood disorder by providing a clear set of steps that can be focused on during emotional storms.

It is important to break down large goals into smaller steps and pick one or two specific actions to complete each step. This provides meaningful direction during times of depressed episodes because it minimizes the problem solving that needs to be done during a mental fog. It also provides grounding during the racing thoughts of a hypomanic state by identifying specific actions to focus on instead of getting caught up in overly embellished possibilities or difficulties.

Example

I again use the example of writing this book. M creativity and effectiveness can be impacted by my moods. I need to have small, specific steps identified so that I can continue to write with direction despite my highs and lows.

My long-term goal was the publishing of this handbook and the short-term goals were the specific chapters. The action steps were put into a template: list activities, explain each activity, and share a personal story with each activity. This provided a specific tangible outline to complete.

Long-Term Goal	Write this book.
Short-Term Goal	Create outline of book.
Action Step	Develop chapter topics.
Action Step	Create activities for each chapter.
Short-Term Goal	Create draft of chapter 1.
Action Step	Outline chapter activities.
Action Step	Provide personal story for each activity.
Action Step	Write explanation for each activity.
Action Step	Proofread chapter.

Exercise

Now it's your turn to dream, to plan, and to achieve. Think of a moderately challenging long term goal that you would like to achieve within the next six months List out the specific steps you need to accomplish to achieve your goal. This process of writing down a structure to follow will provide you with a plan to follow.

Long-Term Goal	
Short-Term Goal	
Action Step	
Action Step	
Action Step	
Short-Term Goal	
Action Step	
Action Step	
Action Step	

Activity 4: Daily Schedule

Instruction

So far we have developed a template of how our physiological and emotional states can flow throughout the day. We have developed long and short term goals with specific actions to achieve them. Now we will start applying the specific action steps into our personalized daily template. A key component in planning a daily routine is to match up the kinds of activities with the state we are in. For example, your most productive time should be reserved for the activities that require problem solving and the most energy. Groggy times such as during medication hangovers are the perfect time to do laundry, dishes, and certain big movement activities because they do not require a lot of thinking. These tasks are heavier work with big movements and help the body work its way through the medication hangover and kick-start the day. Some people may choose to swim or run; others may choose to do laundry or other house chores. The important piece is to choose an activity that satisfies the needs of how you are feeling and supports you in achieving a meaningful objective.

Writing your schedule down lets you see if it's balanced or if you're trying to cram too much in. It's okay if you misjudge the time you think it's going to take to complete something. This is a learning process, and it's a tool to help develop this skill of estimating needed time and resources. Ask any contractor—jobs typically can take more time and be more complicated than originally anticipated. But this should also give you a little bit of freedom because you're working with your body's natural cycle as opposed to trying to force it. Finally, this exercise is not about giving an excuse to not do something; this is about finding tools to support you in doing a couple of things better and more effectively.

Example

I find that I have medication hangovers during the mornings when I am getting ready for the day, especially when I am adjusting a medication change. When first diagnosed with a mood disorder, I had a part-time job in the camping section of a retail store. I was able to schedule my work hours into a second shift. In this way, I had the morning to work through my grogginess and to get ready for work. I did my laundry during that time and found that it helped pull me through my morning grogginess. I'm not saying that everything was wonderful, but I did find that I was better able to perform my job and feel better about my day.

I also identified times to do thinking tasks, such as schoolwork or writing. I had difficulty writing papers during medication hangovers and found studying during that time ineffective and frustrating. However, when I started to plan the studying during more alert times, it became effective. By planning my schedule to match activities with my states, I achieved greater success and reduced stress.

Time	State	Activities	Action Items
7:00 a.m.	Wake up	Wake up	
7:30 a.m.	↑		
8:00 a.m.	**Medication**	Breakfast, shower,	Vacuum living room carpet
8:30 a.m.	**hangover**	walk, clean,	Walk 2 miles
9:00 a.m.	(low-thinking activities)		
9:30 a.m.	↓		
10:00 a.m.	↕	↑	Type 1-2 activities
10:30 a.m.		work on book	
11:00 a.m.	**Most alert**	↓	
11:30 a.m.	(important activities)	Pay bills	Open and organize mail
12:00 p.m.	↓	pay	
12:30 p.m.		Lunch	Make a salad
1:00 p.m.			
1:30 p.m.	↑		
2:00 p.m.	**Tired**	Do laundry, read for pleasure	Put clothes in washing machine
2:30 p.m.	(easy activities)		Read a book
3:00 p.m.	↓		
3:30 p.m.	↑		
4:00 p.m.	**Second wind**	Plan next day, homework,	Study History chapter
4:30 p.m.	(next-important activities)		Do Math assignment
5:00 p.m.			
5:30 p.m.		Cook	
6:00 p.m.	↓	Eat Dinner	
6:30 p.m.	↑		
7:00 p.m.	**Tired**	Listen to music, watch TV	Sit on coach and watch Avengers
7:30 p.m.	(leisure activities)		
8:00 p.m.	↓		
8:30 p.m.	Exhausted	Sleep	

Exercise

So now it is your turn to map out your daily activities by adding specific action items on your personalized daily template. This is not the time to worry about what should be. Nor is it the time to overload the schedule with superhuman expectations. This is a time to identify the key pieces that need to be done, when is most effective, efficient, or productive to do them, and determine specific actions or items needed in order to fulfill the task.

Time	State	Activity	Action Items
5:00 a.m.			
5:30 a.m.			
6:00 a.m.			
6:30 a.m.			
7:00 a.m.			
7:30 a.m.			
8:00 a.m.			
8:30 a.m.			
9:00 a.m.			
9:30 a.m.			
10:00 a.m.			
10:30 a.m.			
11:00 a.m.			
11:30 a.m.			
12:00 p.m.			
12:30 p.m.			
1:00 p.m.			
1:30 p.m.			
2:00 p.m.			
2:30 p.m.			
3:00 p.m.			
3:30 p.m.			
4:00 p.m.			
4:30 p.m.			

Time	State	Activity	Action Items
5:00 p.m.			
5:30 p.m.			
6:00 p.m.			
6:30 p.m.			
7:00 p.m.			
7:30 p.m.			
8:00 p.m.			
8:30 p.m.			
9:00 p.m.			
9:30 p.m.			
10:00 p.m.			
10:30 p.m.			
11:00 p.m.			
11:30 p.m.			

4 Building Relationships

I have regularly been using Albert Mehrabian's 7%-38%-55% rule as a model for how I build a *relationship with myself.* I have no concrete or objective research to affirm this as fact. I am simply sharing this model because it works for me by organizing and giving perspective to the various aspects I deal with in living successfully with a bipolar condition, and I am sharing it for you to use or dismiss as you see fit.

I find that the extreme *passions* I experience associated with my bipolar episodes are the *relationship* among my *thoughts* (7%), my *physiological state* (38%), and the *actions and behaviors* (55%) I choose to engage in to express them. To learn more, I recommend doing an internet search on the key phrase *physiology of emotions.*

I have realized that the inability to channel that *passion* in the right way is a significant source of stress and intensifies the distress of the experience. Developing both a team of people *and* a set of activities that can respect and accommodate the intensity of my *passion* has proven to be a life changer because I no longer need to feel guilty about the swings. I can simply channel them into the appropriate activities to accommodate the needs of the *passion* while pursuing a desired quality of life.

Activity 1: The Acceptance Ladder: My Relationship With Myself

Instruction

Acceptance of your *condition* as a need to accommodate, provides the context on which to build a healthy, balanced, and meaningful life. Because of the volatility associated with a mood disorder, you can find yourself in various emotional states at any given time. The five stages identified here are Curse, Difficult, Is What It Is, Teacher, and finally Gift. Each stage has its own emotions and thoughts.

Curse—this sucks and why me? The intensity is unbearable. The universe and God are against me. Well, maybe this isn't *really* a curse. *Maybe* this is just …

Difficult—ugh, this is hard. It can be such a battle trying to regulate these emotions inside me, tracking when and how they occur, what I need to do to regulate them, and the fact that I can't do things as easily as others. I get I'm not cursed, but this sure as hell isn't fair. Well, maybe this isn't about being fair. *Maybe* this just …

Is what it is—just is … just is. This is just *my* experience of the human condition that I need to navigate, master, and become mature in my approach with. Well, maybe this isn't *just* what I experience. *Maybe* this is a …

Teacher—an opportunity to develop skills and systems to address a need and the emotional stress required to cause a change. Maybe the active pursuit of these skills and systems allows me to grow as a human being. Well, maybe this isn't *just* a teacher. *Maybe* this is a …

Gift—maybe this allows me to express myself in a way that could not be otherwise and provides a unique opportunity for me to develop and share experiential wisdom that can benefit mankind and the lives of those I care about.

Now, if I am in *curse* mode and you tell me I have a gift, I will tell you to go the hell away, you have no *clue* what you are talking about. I *cannot* hear that thought in that mode … not even from myself. What I *can* do, however, is entertain the possibility of the next stage. Then, once I have accepted the new stage, I can entertain the next, and so on. At each stage, I can go one step up or one step down. I get to choose.

Example

Gift	When the pain and chaos subsides, I can find the beauty in simplicity. I never would appreciate things the way I do now if it wasn't for the struggles and chaos I had before. This makes me a better Occupational Therapist.
Teacher	This is a challenge and I am learning to separate myself from how I feel. What skill do I need to focus on learning so I can have what I want?
Is What It Is	Just is … just is. This is just *my* experience of the human condition that I need to navigate, master, and become mature in my approach with.
Difficult	This is so unfair and so difficult. I hate all the tracking and work it takes me to simply get through a day. I hate this thing.
Curse	I can't do this. Everything goes wrong and the pain is unbearable. I can't take this. I have no hope.

Exercise

Identify the current stage you are in. Then, try to develop a perspective for the next stage up … and *only* the next stage up. Once you are able to accept that stage, *then* move on to the next. This isn't about having an answer on how things should be. This is about accepting and addressing with where you *are now* for the *next step*.

Gift	
Teacher	
Is What It Is	
Difficult	
Curse	

Activity 2: The Importance of Boundaries

Instruction

It helps to have safe people around us so we can freely express our moods in its raw volume of *passion* and then help guide us in expressing in appropriate ways when we are lost within our internal storms. It helps to have people around us who can understand the internal pressure and frustration with a mood disorder so that we may have a safe place to be human. These people who help guide us during our internal emotional storms are our *lighthouses*. Not everyone can be a lighthouse, and even those who can be, can't be all the time based on their own moods and needs.

Remember to respect your *lighthouse's* time and space so they can hear the emotional experience behind what you are saying and understand what to do with the intensity in which you share. Twelve people at five minutes each means you get a full sixty minutes of venting *without* draining or overwhelming any one person.

We need to respect the fact that people may not understand what our lived experiences are like. They may not have the emotional space available to process the intensity of how we express ourselves. By establishing preset boundaries we can share our feelings within a context of clear boundaries so the listener can know how to handle the emotional intensity we share.

Example

I have found that a few key people can go a long way in tempering the intensity of an internal emotional storm. Listing out the boundaries I need to respect and the ways I can share in a table gives me an objective reference point when my ability to think objectively is influenced by my episodic state. The following table is an example of how I respect the boundaries of two of my *lighthouses*.

Person and Contact Info	Boundaries to Respect	How I Can Share
Work supervisor	• Time availability at work • To improve work effectiveness, *not* personal therapy session	• Ask if there is time available and how much time before sharing. • Face-to-face in office
Mom	• Has own passions that also need to be heard. • Work schedule and responsibilities	• Call and ask availability and time. • Ongoing text vent of thinking process, *not* complaining

Exercise

Now it is your turn to develop some lighthouses of your own. Build your network by creating and honoring agreed-upon boundaries.

Person and Contact Info	Boundaries to Respect	How I Can Share

Activity 3: Active Listening: How You Are Heard

Instruction

The challenging part about sharing from our difference in thought process is that what can be apparently obvious to us is often seen as irrelevant or unrelated to another person. It can help if we are able to identify the perspective of the listener and then share our thoughts and feelings through the language of that listening. The *skill* that supports that is *active listening*.

Active listening involves providing feeding back of what is heard to confirm our understanding of the meaning behind what was said. This allows the listener to maintain focus on what the other person is saying instead of what we want to say given our next chance to speak.

In chapter 2, "Understanding My Condition," we completed exercises that helped us discern the way we experience the condition for our own understanding. Now we will develop ways to communicate our feelings so that others will better understand us. Improving communication is the key to building strong and healthy relationships

Example

My episodes can make me a very self-centered person because the immediacy and intensity of my emotional needs tend to be overwhelming for me. The vicious trap I fall into is that I have an intensity of emotion that I want/need to share that is atypical. It is difficult for me to express and difficult for the other person understand. When this happens, I am left feeling alone, weird, and misunderstood, while the other person walks away feeling overwhelmed and unable to help. My emotional state intensifies because I have no outlet and the other person is less likely to be available in the future. I get frustrated that people just didn't understand me, leading to an erosion of my confidence.

If I focus *first* on listening and understanding where that person is coming from, I have a better chance of being understood.

Person	His Or Her Interests and Experiences	How I Can Share My Experience
Brother	Football, father of a three-year-old	I must address needs sometimes before I can move on to what I want to do.
Mother	Job coordinates people, develops and implements programs, likes to read	My thinking process, big-picture ideas
Father	Football, an accountant, is Santa at Christmas	Specific actions completed, specific skill being used

Exercise

List out the specific people you have in your life and their interests. Then, list out how you can share your experience and moods in a way that could make sense to them.

Person	His Or Her Interests	How I Can Share My Experience

Activity 4: Service Is the Key

Instruction

There is a connection between our internal thoughts and the state of *passion* that we are currently experiencing. The world just looks different when we are sad versus frustrated versus happy. By having a mission statement we have a point of reference to live life from independent from how we feel.

We can focus on the simple acts that support the joy of another and be present to *his or her* passion. By focusing on the needs and interests of others we can become more aware of the interests of those around us. This isn't about making them understand us better. This is about having a connection, and thus relationship, with others to counter the feelings of isolation during depression, ground the unbridled energy and creativity of mania, and help calm ourselves during the discomfort of anxiety.

Example

The chart below helps me organize and identify the priorities and needs of the important people in my life. This provides a system to guide me in channeling my *passion* during my episodes that allows me to engage in meaningful, relationship-building activities with those around me.

Person	Joys, Passion, and Needs	Ways I Can Help
Mom	Developing projects for work, housework	Help with housework, ask and listen to her progress on her work projects, help with needs around the house
Dad	Football, being Santa for Christmas, difficulty with modern technology	Ask about his Santa experiences, watch football with him, ask about his fantasy football league, be available to help with computer needs, fix chair when it breaks
Brother	Three-year-old daughter, football, politics, economics	Available to babysit niece, help with landscaping around house, discuss topics on politics and economics

Exercise

Now it's your turn. List the important people in your life are their areas of interest and needs. Then list the specific ways you can provide them support.

Person	Joys, Passion, and Needs	Ways I Can Help

5 General Finances

Finance is a real issue. It is a tool, a prison, a trap, and an opportunity all at the same time. Finances need to be respected. We have varying relationships with money. Some people hate the concept of finance and see it as an enemy. Others love the concept of money and revel in it. As with all things, a healthy balance between the two is invaluable.

I find that things are always more overwhelming when they're disorganized. The act of gathering information and putting it all in one place can be a very empowering and relieving task once it's completed. This task itself may feel very confronting, challenging, and frightening; but breaking it down into small exercises will make the process more manageable. When all of the information is gathered in one place, it becomes easier to make choices and decisions because we have an accurate picture of what's going on. All too often we make financial decisions based on how we feel and are unaware of the long-term repercussions of that decision.

This chapter is designed to provide a template to demystify the potentially overwhelming responsibility of money. The completion of the activities in this chapter will provide a very strong foundation for further discussions with a financial planner.

Activity 1: Get It All on One Page

(Part 1: Current Funds)

Instruction

Organizing our finances helps to demystify our notions about money. This first section is for gathering all the information of where we have money (checking accounts, savings accounts, stocks, etc.) By creating a master sheet with the names and contact information of the institutions, type of accounts, account numbers, and all other relevant information we take an important step to manage our finances. With a mood disorder our thinking is not always objective, often causing rash, impulsive spending rather than following a budgetary plan.

Example

I never liked dealing with finances. I find it this overwhelming thing that has a direct impact on me. With my bipolar condition, I have days where I feel like everything will work out okay (hypomania), so therefore I can take risks. I have other days where I can't think my way out of a box (depression), which can turn those previous financial opportunities into apparent obstacles. I need to simplify my financial situation by finding a manageable plan that makes sense when experiencing either a manic or depressed episode.

Before I set this up, I used to find that I got tired of just trying to figure out where to get the information I need in order to make a decision. My list helps me see the reality of my financial situation which makes it easier to decide on future spending.

Financial Institution Information	Account Type	Account Number	Interest	Balance
Federal Credit Union 88 Main St, Somewhere, NY 88888				
Member Number: xxxxxxxx	Checking	xx-xxxx	.01%	$xxx.xx
Phone Number: 888-888-8888	Savings	xx-xxxx	1.1%	$xxx.xx

Financial Institution Information	Account Type	Account Number	Interest	Balance
Bank 99 Main St, Somewhere Else, NY 99999				
Member Number: yyyyyyyyyyy	Checking	xx-xxxx	0%	$xxx.xx
Phone Number: 999-999-9999	Savings	xx-xxxx	1.2%	$xxx.xx

Exercise

List your checking, savings, IRAs, stocks, and other financial accounts on one page. Include account numbers, institution addresses and phone numbers.

Financial Institution Information	Account Type	Account Number	Interest	Balance

Financial Institution Information	Account Type	Account Number	Interest	Balance

(Part 2: Current Loans)

Instruction

Debt is a double-edged sword. When managed correctly, it can provide opportunity. When mismanaged, it becomes a prison, a source of stress, or an obstacle one has to fight against. This section will help you understand the situation and will later be used as a tool. It's important that we have an awareness of our debt-to-income ratio because creditors use it to determine our financial health. We all have multiple forms of debt (credit cards, car loans, student loans, mortgage, etc.) and it is easy to lose track of where our true financial health lies.

Example

I get uncomfortable when I see my debt listed on one page. Through my manic times, I feel like every opportunity will work. I think I can make credit-based purchases to set up income-based projects because in my mind everything is going to work out. When I am depressed, I can't keep the creativity and energy going that is required to pursue my goals. Even if the income-producing opportunity dries up, the debt and responsibility I used to begin the project did not. By listing all my loans on one page and seeing the total amount, I made myself see the reality of my debt. Even though this exercise was uncomfortable in the beginning, it was actually freeing once I had a structure in place to address my debt. Disorganization is very difficult to manage, so getting my financial situation on one list allowed me to start working with it.

Institution Information	Account Type	Account Number	Interest	Balance
Federal Credit Union Member Number: 2032 Somewhere Rd. Webster, NY 12345 Phone: 585-123-4567	Car loan Mortgage	xxxxxxx xxxxxxx	10% 4.5%	$xx,xxx $xxx,xxx

Exercise

List your outstanding loans. Write down the specific name, address, contact information, account number, interest, and balance for each account. This information will be used to create a foundation for financial freedom and accurately plan for a healthy financial future.

Institution Information	Account Type	Account Number	Interest	Balance

(Part 3: Income Sources)

Instruction

Knowing your expected income per paycheck, per month, and per year from all sources helps us see the whole picture instead of looking at one income check at a time. In this way, our projected annual income can be seen as a source of hope for clearing loans and planning future savings and spending.

Example

When I first made this list, I found it was very short. I had one job where I was paid biweekly, and my sources of income compared to my debt looked a little daunting. At the same time, though, it was grounding to know what I actually had to work with.

Employer Information	Payment Type	Average Pay Period	Average Monthly	Average Yearly
Sales Associate				
Some Outdoors Store	Hourly	410	820	10,660
2032 Somewhere Rd. Webster, NY 12345	Paid biweekly			
Phone: 444-444-4444				
SSI	1st Wednesday of month		$x,xxx	$xx,xxx

Exercise

Now complete your list of income sources, contact information, pay frequency and amounts. Use averages and round down to the nearest five dollars for ease of numbers.

Income Source	Payment Type	Average Pay Period	Average Monthly	Average Yearly

(Part 4: Bills)

Instruction

This section is where we list out our bills. Now the difference between bills and debt is that debt can eventually be paid off. Loans, mortgages, and credit cards all have a dollar amount that if you consistently pay can actually reach zero. Bills (cell phone, car insurance, electricity, gym memberships, water, etc.), on the other hand, will never be paid off because you will always be using the item and thus always have to pay for it.

Example

This section really started to make sense to me when I was on my own and had to pay for my own utilities. It helped me see how I was spending money. Later on when we create our financial plan, you'll see where the weight of your spending is. It will also show you how much freer you will be when all you have are your bills.

Institution Information	Account Type	Account Number	Monthly Payment
Verizon	Cell Phone	xxxx-xxx	80
Member Number: xxx-xxx-xxxx			
2032 Somewhere Rd. Somewhere, NY 12345			
Phone: 222-222-2222			

Exercise

List the companies that bill you each month with their contact information, account numbers, and monthly amounts. Some may vary, like a gas bill being more in the winter than in the summer. With these, find an average, or just use the highest one all the time. I try to use the higher one so I build in some slush money for unexpected situations.

Institution Information	Account Type	Account Number	Monthly Payment

Activity 2: Budget

Instruction

Financial plans only work when they deal with reality. Now that we have all the various types of information, we need to get a sense of how we actually use it. Once spending has been tracked for two or three months, then we can come up with a realistic approach for budget planning based on actual spending habits, lifestyle, and responsibilities.

Example

I find that the easiest way to keep track of my spending is through using my debit card for purchases. One of my bank's online features is a budget section. I simply go online and assign each purchase to a category. I then look at my total spending to get an idea of where my money goes.

Exercise

Below is a table to use for itemizing your spending each week for a month. First, track spending for each week for a month and then complete that list for two or three months to get a realistic sense of how you spend your money. Fill out each subcategory individually and place the total in the shaded area of the category.

	Budgeted	Week 1	Week 2	Week 3	Week 4
Savings					
Rent or Mortgage					
Utilities					
Gas/Oil					
Electric					
Cable					
Phone					
Internet					
Cell					
Garbage					

	Budgeted	Week 1	Week 2	Week 3	Week 4
Medical					
Insurance					
Doctor					
Meds					
Dentist					
Car					
Car loan					
Insurance					
Vehicle gas					
Vehicle maintenance					
Registration					
Inspection					
Groceries					
Food					
Household Maintenance					
Eat out					
Clothes					
Entertainment					
Memberships					
Discretionary					
Vacation					
Kids					
Activity 1					
Activity 2					
Activity 3					
Activity 4					
Other					
School loans					
Credit cards					
Fees					
Total expenses					

Activity 3: Establishing Accounts

Instruction

Financial stability is an important factor for healthy living because of the stress caused by the mismanagement of funds. Now that we know what we have, how much money we get, how much money we owe, and how we spend, we can now create a structure and system that supports our current situation and lifestyle. It is important to create an external structure that supports us in managing our financial responsibilities during a chaotic internal emotional state. If our financial picture is only in thought, it can easily shift based on our mood during a given emotional situation.

Example

Lots of money in one place inevitably gets me in trouble. I find it hard to manage large amounts of money when given multiple demands. I set up a structure as a way to cut down the amount of money I have to think about at any given time. This limits the accessibility to funds which protects my money from myself. Having money easily accessible makes life easier, but it is also easier to mess up my situation through a manic spending splurge. The more steps I have to go through to get money, the more opportunities I have to say no to a spending urge.

I have my check deposited into my bills account and I transfer a budgeted amount of money into another account for short-term/fun things (e.g., gas, food, going out to dinner or a movie) accessible with a debit card. Then I only have a specific amount of money easily available at a given time. I may have more money elsewhere, but it is already spoken for. Less money to manage helps show me what I actually have to spend and forces me to stay within my budget.

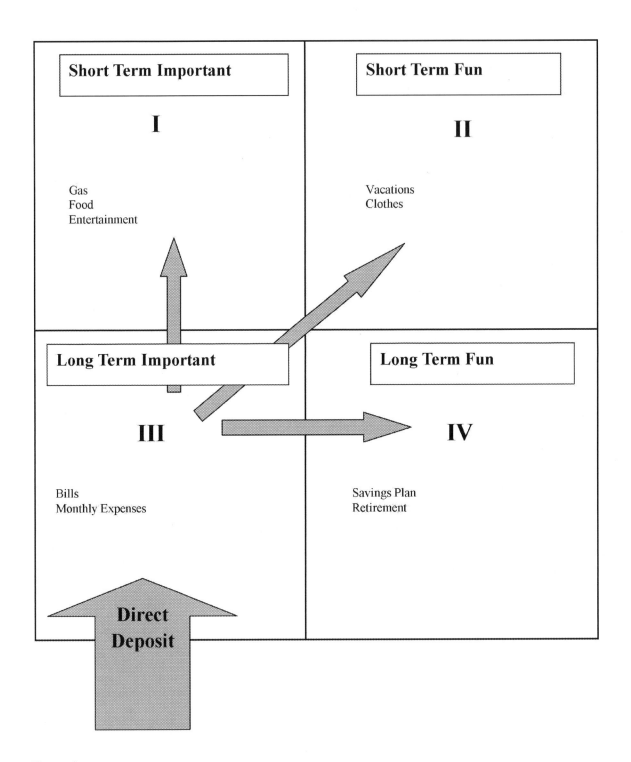

Checking

Savings

Short Term Important	Short Term Fun
I	**II**
Gas Food Entertainment	Vacations Clothes

Long Term Important	Long Term Fun
III	**IV**
Bills Monthly Expenses	Savings Plan Retirement

Direct Deposit

Exercise

Create your accounts at your own bank. Be sure to update your account information if you are adding new accounts

Activity 4: Climbing out of Debt

Instruction

Debt sucks! Long after the quick joys of an opportunity or toy have diminished, the responsibility of the expense lasts. Debt is a tool, and just like fire or a loaded gun, it can be very destructive if mismanaged. This section will distinguish *bills* from *debt*. In this activity, a set amount of money will be dedicated to paying bills and a set amount of money will be established to paying off debt. By creating a sustainable plan to pay off debt, we create a lifestyle that is based on financial reality.

I found this a very freeing exercise and actually learned about it from John Cummuta's *Transforming Debt into Wealth*, Robert Kiyosaki's *Rich Dad, Poor Dad*, and a Paying Off Debt app for my smart phone. List out your minimum payments per loan and commit an extra amount to the process (John Commuta's *Transforming Debt into Wealth System* refers to it as the accelerator margin). The total of these becomes your budgeted monthly debt-payoff amount. When the first loan is paid off, roll the money previously committed into another loan. In this way, we pay down our loans faster and faster. When completed, there is a great sense of freedom available. We become able to use our money to build our own dreams and lifestyle instead of renting our lifestyles from lenders.

Example

I am no expert in financial matters and found myself staring bankruptcy in the face after medical bills and a couple of hypomanic-influenced spending decisions. Before I did this exercise, I felt trapped, scared of the large amount of debt that I had accumulated in my journey of trying to figure out how to live with my diagnosis. I didn't have a rich uncle to bail me out, and I had to figure it out on my own. The value is that while the situation had difficult challenging times, it taught me a way to look at money and objects that helped me comprehend the long-term impact. I entered my various bills and debt into the chart below and developed my plan to climb out of debt.

Bills	Amount	Date	Payment Type
Rent	750	1	Check
Cell phone	80	15	*Auto* pay credit card
Car insurance	130	20	*Auto* pay credit card

Bills	Amount	Date	Payment Type
Life insurance	60	20	*Auto* pay bank
Other	80		*Auto* pay credit card
Subtotal	**1,100**		

Debt	Interest	Minimum Payment	Date	Payment Type	Balance
Home appliance	6%	125	5	*Auto* pay bank	2,350
Car	12%	200	1	*Auto* pay bank	12,000
School loans	7%	220	28	*Auto* pay bank	40,000
Credit card 1	15%	100	1	Self pay	8,000
Credit card 2	15%	65	15	Self pay	5,000
Credit card 3	15%	25	28	Self pay	2,000
Subtotal		**735**			**69,350**
Extra		**100**			

Exercise

Take your bills and loans listed in the previous sections and place them in the charts below. Once these are established, it becomes far easier to follow a plan because you only need to track your short-term fun money. The system takes care of the rest.

Unending Bills	Amount	Date	Payment Type
Subtotal			

Ending Bills	Interest	Minimum Payment	Date	Payment Type	Balance

Subtotal

Extra

Appendix

Some posts from my blog: http://sharingthejourney.postagon.com/

These posts are to provide an example of the *thought process* I use to implement the tools shared in this book. Remember, this is not about having the right information. This is about experiencing a desired quality of life *with* the strong emotional experiences of the episodes. As such, I submit my thoughts and perspectives as a resource for you to agree, disagree, relate to, or discredit to support the development of your own.

- **Resiliency**
- **Do You Believe?**
- **The Gift of the Condition**
- **Personal Soundtrack**

Helpful Resources

This section lists various books and other resources that I have found supportive in developing a lifestyle to successfully live with my bipolar condition.

Resiliency

Al Siebert, PhD, talks about resiliency in his books *The Resiliency Advantage* and *The Survivor Personality*. I have found resiliency is a vital skill in successfully living with a bipolar disorder. Remember how I shared about how an uncontrolled release of *passion* breaks down boundaries? (See blog "Boundaries and the Incas.") Every time I recovered from an episodic state (and my presentation is rapid cycling, so it can be a few hours to a few months), I had a mess to reorganize and new boundaries to construct, and I felt like I was in a constant state of starting over. Now that I have a personal mission statement (see blog "My Mission Creates My Boundaries"), my boundaries are more durable, meaning that I am able to experience a sense of personal consistency *during* the internal emotional storms consistent with a bipolar episode. This was developed using resiliency.

Seibert shared the following "Eight Principles Affecting Your Resiliency" (*The Resiliency Advantage*, p. 32).

1. When hit by a life-disrupting change (which an episode can easily and often be), you will never be the same.
2. As you struggle with adversity or disruptive change, your mind and habits will create barriers or bridges to a better future.
3. Blaming others for how bad things are for you keeps you in a nonresilient victim state, in which you do not take resiliency actions.
4. Life isn't fair, and that can be good for you.
5. Your unique resiliency strengths develop from self-motivated, self-managed learning in the school of life.
6. Self-knowledge enhances your resiliency because your way of being resilient must be your own self-created, unique version. Self-knowledge comes from self-observation, experimenting, and being receptive to feedback of all kinds.
7. The observing place within you is where you develop conscious choices about how you will interact with the world you live in. Experiencing choices leads to feelings of freedom, independence, and being in control of your life.
8. As you become more and more resilient, you effectively handle disruptive change, adversities, and major setbacks faster and easier.

Check out Nick Vujicic's YouTube video. He explains this far better than I *ever* could.

The video can be seen at http://www.youtube.com/watch?v=AJvEoLPLIg8

Do You Believe?

Believe you can, believe you can't, either way you're right.
—Henry Ford

Do you believe?

I'm too tired for this right now ...

Do you believe?

Believe in what—that I have a mental illness? Yes, I do. And it's a pain in the butt with the extremes I go through and the work it takes to get through the day sometimes.

Do you believe?

Believe in *what* exactly? My rapid-cycling physiological state of *passion* can shift on a dime, causing my perspective to constantly shift. I feel like I'm always losing my grounding.

Do you believe?

Why am I stuck with this? I *hate* this. This isn't fair!

Do you believe?

I want an answer. I want to know why I have this. I want to know how to live with this. I want to live a life that makes me happy without dealing with all this internal crap that people just don't seem to get. I want to feel normal and shed the ache of isolation that comes from feeling wrong and sick and broken. I want to enjoy my life!

Do you believe?

Arggggggggggggg! Believe in what? That something is going to take this pain and emptiness away? That something is going to help me feel whole? That I will be cured of this chronic illness that constantly rears its ugly head, just when I think things are starting to be okay again?

Do you believe?

In what? That somehow, just somehow this will all make sense? That there actually *is* a way to this? That I *can* have a life I enjoy? That there exists the possibility of a life of joy and fulfillment amid this aching storm? *I want this thing to go away!*

Do you believe?

I'm tired. I want to know how to do this. I'm scared that the other shoe is going to drop and that I'm just going to be in another emotional yard sale trying to pick the pieces of my life up and have to piece it all back together *again*.

Do you believe?

But other people are smarter.

Do you believe?

But I'm broken, sick, and crazy. I'm one of *those* people who act funny, are unstable, and thus dangerous. I'm not sure I even trust *myself*.

Do you believe?

Maybe.

Do you believe?

What? I said maybe already.

Do you believe?

Stop. I don't want to do this anymore. I just want to sleep.

Do you believe?

This isn't going to stop, is it?

Do you believe?

(Sigh) In what? That there is a way I *can* do this?

Do you believe?

Maybe.

Do you believe?

I don't know; maybe there is. I guess I've made it *this* far anyway.

Do you believe?

But I don't have a lot of money.

Do you believe?

I guess things have been showing up. I have a job. I have been able to get through some dark days without having to stay in bed all day.

Do you believe?

I *do* know how to stay in mindful action during a preferred activity now. I *do* know how my thoughts can influence my feelings, choices, and behaviors … and that I can choose thoughts to think/focus on.

Do you believe?

I *can* say my thankful ABCs *anytime* I choose. I *can* become mindful of the sensations in my body *anytime* I choose. I *can* give myself permission to be imperfect. I *can* see that many tools and life skills exist to support me in accommodating my needs. I *can* choose my actions. I *can* see that other people who have this have been able to do things that they want to do. I *can* see that people are ready, willing, and able to teach me when I am ready to learn.

Do you believe?

I don't always like how this feels, though.

Do you believe?

I guess.

Do you believe?

Really? We are still doing this? I said I guess already!

Do you believe?

(Sigh) Yes …

Do you believe?

All right, yes.

Do you believe?

I said yes!
....
What?

Do you believe?

The Gift of the Condition

Today being Christmas, I commit to the association with my bipolar condition as a gift. Comfortable? *God, no.* Preferred? *Not a chance.* Yet today, I *choose* it as a gift nonetheless. Why? *Because I have it regardless.*

Cognitive Behavioral Therapy—Situation—thoughts—feelings—actions—situation …

Mindfulness: Emptiness in the center of my chest, nervousness with vulnerability. Feel the pressure of the seat on my bum, the hardness of the desk under my right elbow, and the edge of the laptop on my left wrist as I type. Listening to personal soundtrack and Christmas music to center myself around the theme of the holiday. Scratch my head from an itch, tension in back as I slump a bit while typing.

Personal Soundtrack: Playing on computer as I type. "Little Drummer Boy" by Pentatonix right now actually …

Thankful ABCs: **A**—apple, apple pie, tastes good with ice cream. **B**—brothers, I have two cool ones. **C**—cats, I like the feel of them when they are curled up in my lap. **D**—dog, had a great one growing up. His name was Morgan. **E**—elephant. Why elephant? No idea, popped into head while typing. I like the trunk, though. **F**—not appropriate thing to type about here. **G**—*God*, yes, I believe, even with the struggles. **H**—happiness, it exists, no matter how distant it may seem at times. **I**—ice cream, vanilla with melted peanut butter, love it. **J**—Jenny, name of a couple of women I have found myself loving during my life … and love is good. **K**—kindergarteners, very fun to be with and love their perspectives on life. **L**—love, as I said, love is good, even if it doesn't end the way you originally envisioned. **M**—monkeys, oo oo ah ah, just fun. **N**—nonsense, fun to have some. **O**—orange, the color of a sunset, God's painting in the sky. **P**—playing music, my personal soundtrack and enjoying how it makes me feel. **Q**—Qubert, a video game growing up with a funny character. **R**—Rascal Flatts and their song "Stand" and amazing message that continues to support me. **S**—not appropriate to type about in this venue ☺. **T**—typing this blog and the outlet it provides. **U**—universe of limitless abundance if I am willing to look, listen, and appreciate. **V**—victory, the place I am living from. **W**—wonder, what I get to enjoy when I stop trying to have the answer. **X**—xylophone … I don't know why, started with an X. **Y**—because…. **Z**—zebra, is it black with white stripes or white with black stripes? I wonder.

Current Feelings: Mixed, hollowness, *and* now thankfulness present, motivated toward purpose, humbled by responsibility of actions.

Meaningful Actions: Type blog, take a shower to enjoy the warm water on my skin, work on book—gives my life experience purpose in service to another, spend time with family this afternoon and enjoy being in their company.

Situation: Up, living a chosen and desired quality of life *with* my current emotional state.

Merry Christmas—It's what I celebrate. I share with you the *gift* of the peace and joy I am currently experiencing *with* the *passions* of a bipolar experience. If you celebrate a different holiday, then please apply this to the one *you* have nearest to this occasion. If you are not celebrating anything, then please enjoy this as an exchange of *passion* between human beings who understand the challenges we can all face in life and the values added by celebration and gratitude to spice up the experience.

Personal Soundtrack

Explanations of each song choice are individual posts on my blog:
sharingthejourney.postagon.com.

"Stand"—Rascal Flatts
"Little Drummer Boy"—Pentatonix
"New Soul"—Yael Naim
"Be OK"—Ingrid Michaelson
"100 Years"—Five for Fighting
"For the Love of a Princess"—Myleene Kiss
"Honor Him", "Elysium", "Now We Are Free"—Gladiator Soundtrack (by Hans Zimmer)
"Somewhere over the Rainbow"—Israel Kamakawiwo'ole
"What a Wonderful World"—Louis Armstrong

What is important is that *you* select songs that connect with *your passion*, not limiting yourself to my songs. If they work, great! Use them, but don't limit yourself to them. The power is in the customized connection to *your* passion.

Helpful Resources

Books

Beers, M. H. (2006). *The Merck Manual of Diagnosis and Therapy, 18th Edition.* Whitehouse Station: Merck Research Laboratories.

Carnegie, D. (1936). *How to Win Friends & Influence People.* New York: Simon & Schuster.

Copeland, M. E. (2010). *WRAP Plus.* Dummerston: Peach Press.

Covey, S. R. (1990). *7 Habbits of Highly Effective People.* New York: Simon & Schuster.

Dowd, T., & Tierney, J. (2005). *Teaching Social Skills to Youth, 2nd Edition.* Boys Town: Boys Town Press.

Johnson, S. M. (1998). *Who Moved My Cheese.* New York: Putnum Adult.

Kiosaki, R., & Letcher, S. (2000). *Rich Dad Poor Dad.* New York: Warner Books.

Kuhnke, E. (2012). *Body Language for Dummies, 2nd Edition.* Chichester, West Sussex: John Wiley & Sons, Ltd.

Seibert, A. P. (2005). *The Resiliency Advantage.* San Francisco: Berrett-Koehler Publishers, Inc.

Websites

Cognitive Behavioral Therapy Self-Help Resources: http://www.getselfhelp.co.uk/freedownloads2.htm

Depression Bipolar Support Alliance: http://www.dbsalliance.org

John Commuta's Transforming Debt into Wealth Course: http://www.johncummuta.com

Nick Vujicic's YouTube video: http://www.youtube.com/watch?v=V6vFVFlRaPY#t=10

TRUE DIRECTIONS

An affiliate of Tarcher Books

OUR MISSION

Tarcher's mission has always been to publish books
that contain great ideas. Why? Because:

GREAT LIVES BEGIN WITH GREAT IDEAS

At Tarcher, we recognize that many talented authors, speakers, educators,
and thought-leaders share this mission and deserve to be published –
many more than Tarcher can reasonably publish ourselves. True
Directions is ideal for authors and books that increase awareness, raise
consciousness, and inspire others to live their ideals and passions.

Like Tarcher, True Directions books are designed to do three things:
inspire, inform, and motivate.

Thus, True Directions is an ideal way for these important voices to
bring their messages of hope, healing, and help to the world.

Every book published by True Directions– whether it is non-fiction, memoir,
novel, poetry or children's book – continues Tarcher's mission to publish works
that bring positive change in the world. We invite you to join our mission.

For more information, see the True Directions website:
www.iUniverse.com/TrueDirections/SignUp

Be a part of Tarcher's community to bring positive change in this world!
See exclusive author videos, discover new and exciting books, learn about
upcoming events, connect with author blogs and websites, and more!
www.tarcherbooks.com